I0464415

2015 Businesses

Learn and re-learn what makes businesses succeed, grow and survive

Ian Juul

Copyright © 2015 Ian Juul
All rights reserved.

ISBN-13: 978-1511761109
ISBN-10: 1511761105

Contents

Preface

Businesses - we all have regular contact with them. We buy goods and services from them, we work in them and we work for them. We may even own one. We all need them and we rely on them for our day to day existence. We also invest in them for our retirement income and we rely of them in legacy planning.

The core principles of business are generic across the world, irrespective of the geographies, languages, currencies, governments, cultures, climates and business environments. All businesses are linked with the same common principles.

Being a good manager, executive or business owner requires special skills. You can study, learn and apply business theory and principles to a certain point but the truly **exceptional** managers, executives and business owners all have a special instinctive quality. They just 'know' what to do 99 % of the time.

Understanding the theory and principles of business is the easy part. Execution is the differentiator.

Please enjoy the book and I sincerely hope it makes you a better Manager.

If you have any experiences or questions please email me on ian@2015businesses.com

I have personally consulted to an estimated 2,000 businesses and I have owned 15 of my own businesses in 5 different countries.

Ian Juul
May 2015

Chapter 1

What is Business – The Basics

Your home is a business

There are many similarities between managing a family home and managing a business. The table below illustrates some of them. If you can manage a home, then you have the potential to manage in a business. A host of common principles and practices apply to both. The difference between success and failure lies in your ability to manage.

Home	Common factors	Business
Income derives from family salaries and wages	**Income sources**	Income derives from sales
There are household expenses such as rent, groceries, transport, telephone, education, medical and debt repayments.	**Overheads and expenses**	There are Overheads such as payroll, rent, inventory, transport, telephone, utilities and debt repayments.
This is the cash left after salaries and wages have paid for home expenses. This surplus cash should be saved, although a large portion is	**Profit and savings**	This is cash left after sales and incomes income have paid cost of goods sold (inventory) and overheads. Profits are usually paid-out

normally spent on luxury goods and 'nice' things like vacations.		to owners and some are reinvested into the business for growth, reducing debts and creating opportunities.
Personal loans, study loans, credit cards, vehicle loans	**Debt**	Credit lines, investor and institutional loans, credit cards
To purchase assets (homes, cars etc) and 'nice' things and sometimes used to pay for monthly expenses like groceries, which is a bad thing.	**Uses of debt**	To expand and grow and leverage opportunities, to purchase assets (real estate, equipment) and sometimes to fund cash-flows.
When expenses exceed income	**Losses**	When expenses exceed income
'Your boss': the employer who purchases your skills, time and loyalty and maybe your greater Community	**Customers**	Clients (including other businesses) who buy your goods and services and the greater Community
Individuals or shops from which you buy goods and services you need in order to run your home	**Suppliers**	Individuals or other firms from which you buy goods and services needed to run your own business
Family members perform specific	**Systems and governance**	Owners, managers and staff have

tasks in order to assist with the smooth running of the home. There are house rules		specific tasks and there are certain ways in which duties are performed. There are rules
Salary and wage slips, grocery slips, invoices, vouchers, bank statements, credit card slips, medical reports. These are usually filed for future reference	**Records and filing**	Sales information, invoices, bank statements, salary information, performance reports, business intelligence, compliance records. These are all filed for future reference.
Controls are in place, usually as required by government. These include registering births and deaths, having licenses, paying taxes	**Legal requirements**	Formal controls include registering businesses, hiring employees, financial activities, licenses, foreign trading, tax assessments
Family members share 'ownership' of the family, usually parents holding control and other members having varying degrees of influence	**Ownership**	Individuals or other businesses that have legally registered ownership in the form of agreements, stock certificates
Each family has a legal name, physical home address,	**Identity**	Each business has a legal name, a trading trade, a physical

contact telephone numbers		address, e-mail signatures, website, contact numbers
Each home has a peculiar style and manner, characterized by different behaviors, values, morals and religious beliefs. These qualities are often an extension of the parents' personalities and beliefs with influences from others	**Culture**	Each business conducts itself in a unique manner, characterized by varying degrees of professionalism, service levels, and a presence. Usually an extension of the owners' and managers personalities, beliefs and management styles
Important decisions are usually made and enforced by the parents, with influences from others	**Management process**	Important decisions are usually made by owners and managers and they are enforced downwards through the hierarchy
Usually from parents to children. There can be competition to improve position within the overall 'pecking order'. The hierarchy may evolve as responsibilities change and over	**Hierarchy of leadership**	A well-defined hierarchy from owners through managers to staff. The structure is determined by level of responsibility, skill, formal and informal power, politics and

time		influencers. Roles may change and evolve.
In most cases decisions are made by the parents, often relying on information supplied by family members	**Decisions making process**	Usually made by owners and management, often relying on information supplied by the staff and systems
There is daily conflict, mostly low level and safe. Extreme conflict breaks-down family bonds and is destructive.	**Conflict**	Not every-one agrees with everything all the time. Some conflict is healthy but it needs to be well managed.
Family members are the 'staff' in the sense that they have tasks and roles to fulfill. Some families have paid staff	**Staff**	People are employed by the owners or managers to perform certain tasks and roles and to get daily work done
Family home	**Premises and physical location**	Factory, shop or trading site
A planned addition to the family, the acquisition of a bigger home or the accumulation of more assets	**Growth**	Hiring more staff, acquiring more assets, increased sales, more business volume, more activity
A significant change in the home, such as	**Termination**	When the business ceases to trade for

a death or divorce, or a child leaving to start their home		any reason or it is absorbed into another business or when it undergoes a material 'change'.

How big is your business?

Generally speaking, businesses can be broadly categorized in size as follows:

Large   Has several owners, usually other businesses
Lends money from large banks and formal institutions
Has a very large (wide and deep) management structure
Managers are well educated, often with high degrees
Decisions and implementing changes take a long time
There are multitudes of written rules and policies
The business relies heavily on systems to get work done
There are multiple product lines and income streams
Achieves growth through acquisitions ie. Buying other businesses
Has a large geographical footprint
Has 1000's of employees
Has been in business for decades

Medium   Has several owners
Has a large management structure
May transition into a larger business, if correctly funded and managed
Has less than 1000 employees

Isn't a Small or Large business

Small   Has one or a few owners
Has a small and flat management structure
Lends very little money and relies on owners for funding
Managers and owners may not have many degrees or formal educations
Decisions are made and implemented quickly
There are few written rules and policies but most policies are verbal
Might transition into a Medium sized business but probably won't
Relies on people to get work done and systems are scarce
Has a few products and limited income streams
Grows through adding new products and service lines
Has a small geographical footprint
Has less than 250 employees
Has been in business less than 10 years

Micro   A one-man business, such as street vendor / hawker
Survivalist type business, often found in developing countries where poverty and unemployment is high
The owner is the business, the manager and probably has no staff
Funded by very small own funds, literally a few hundreds of dollars – at most
Frequently changes product and service lines
Very mobile and moves locations frequently

Be in business to stay in business. That's how you create value.

Some features of modern business

Businesses in general share similar characteristics and many face the same challenges.

Entrepreneurial spirit

Most business owners, executives and manager have an incredibly high level of motivation, optimism and a desire to succeed. They love doing business and they have a strong passion for it. Entrepreneurial spirit is what creates and leverages opportunities. All great nations have a high degree of entrepreneurial spirit.

Limited funds

Most businesses are under-capitalized and would like more money, to assist easing daily cash-flow pressures, to leveraging opportunities and to grow. This lack of funding is usually because businesses are unable to secure funds from lenders and they rely heavily on owners to fund the business. Formal lenders generally view businesses as a high-risk market, especially small and medium-sized businesses. With more funds being available to businesses to borrow, economies would be stronger and unemployment would be lower.

Competitive markets

The majority of businesses trade within competitive markets. These markets are typified by a large number of competitors, tight and low margins and low growth rates. With globalization, competition is increasing and markets are getting disrupted whilst some new ones are created but these are usually first leveraged by larger businesses. New technologies and the emerging countries middle classes are exciting growth markets. However, the world is getting smaller and there is more competitive. Foreign markets take time to understand and local protectionism in various forms makes leveraging foreign markets difficult.

Pressures to be leaner and faster

The need to get leaner, work faster, employ less people, leverage machine capacity, simplify processes, reduce costs and squeeze everything so tight that it nearly breaks is a growing trend. Small percentages are now BIG gains. We are running-out of NEW things to do and improve upon.

Conglomerates

Larger businesses are increasingly relying on mergers and acquisitions as a growth strategy. This means some markets are more easily influenced by a collective few.

Diminishing primary resources

Primary resources are getting scarcer. Virgin markets are scarcer. 'Cheap' labor is slowly getting more expensive. Real estate is getting more expensive. The number of developing countries is getting smaller. There is more and more activity happening in a closed container that can only accommodate so much.

Failure rate

Repetitive studies indicate that an estimated 80% of businesses fail within five years of starting up. Lack of funding and a lack of management skills are identified as two of the major reasons for this high rate of failure. Most other businesses fail due to poor management. Good management can turn a bad business into a good one and bad management can turn a good business into a bad one.

Labor markets

Smaller businesses are generally more labor intensive than larger ones. This means that smaller businesses get work done using more people than larger businesses do. Processes are replacing people and cheaper payroll markets are increasingly attractive.

Developing countries are being used to manufacture cheaper products. Managers are getting younger and seasoned experience is being diluted and lost. Length of service in a job is getting shorter and employee turnover rates are increasing. Staff retention is a growing global challenge and the number of contractors and free-lancers are growing as this brings less cost to the Employer. More retirees need to work beyond traditional retirement age as retirement financial planning has shortfalls and personal saving levels are diminishing. Skill shortages seem to be widening and this conflicts unemployment growth.

World wide web

More and more information and data is being shared on the www than ever before. Connectivity and access to www and opportunities around this are exponential. Printed materials are phasing-out and digital is growing. The younger generations are influenced as digital technologies re-define purchasing behaviors, human relationships, music, love, careers, information, social media etc. Retail is changing. Cross-border trade regulations are getting fuzzy as controlling the fast-morphing internet gets harder and harder for the authorities. Hacking, spyware, GPS, adware and software variants grow daily. Virtual currencies are emerging, money laundering is more topical and old-fashioned bartering may return again as the perception of financial 'value' changes.

Faster pace

Life is getting quicker, business is getting quicker and the pace just seems to get faster and faster. If you don't keep up, you fall behind and you lose touch. New trends form, some die and some morph again into a new direction. It takes a lot of effort and concentration 'staying in the game'. To be good you have to work harder, longer and smarter than ever before and the pace is not letting-up. It is intense.

Truth

Dictators, lies and spies are less tolerated. The world wants more truth and transparency. Businesses and business people that are not 'truthful' will be suffer. Whistle-blowers are modern heroes and there are growing intolerances towards abusing natural resources, abusing people and animals, abusing privacy, touching dirty money, too much government, too much power, too much control etc. Honest truthful Leaders know the way forward and this includes business. People are getting tired of the Spin Doctors and 'BS' is rightfully being challenged.

Chapter 2

Risk

The risk profile

Risk is the probability / likelihood of an event or occurrence taking place that has a negative and detrimental influence over your current or planned activities. Risk can be avoided or mitigated through planning.

Every person has a defined tolerance level towards risk and the tolerance may vary depending on the situation and the 'worst case' scenario. If 'worst case' scenario is a soft / low cost outcome, then higher risks may be acceptable. If 'worst case' scenario has a hard / high cost outcome, then lower risks will be sought. What is 'low risk' and what is 'high risk' differs between people. What is very risky to one person might be acceptable to another. Your level of risk tolerance will affect the decisions you make and your level of your authority and influence on the business will influence the risks the business will take.

The economic principle of 'high risk equals high return' means that a high risk can be taken when the potential returns are justifiable. What is a high risk and an acceptably high return will differ from person to person, yet the principle should be remembered.

Risk profile can also change depending on certain factors like moods, emotions, desperation, urgency etc. A risk you take today may not be taken tomorrow as circumstances and experiences change the risk decision and profile. When environments are stable and comfortable, the mood for risk abates. When the environment is unstable, unpredictable, hard and possibly desperate, then the demand needs for risk taking increase.

Businesses work in risk 24/7 and you need to be conscious of your 'risk tolerance'. Statistically, taking too many risks (dicing the odds) will lead to failure. Similarly, playing it safe with continual low risks may lead to an under-performance. A balance needs to be sought and the success of striking the right balance will depend on a number variables, one of which is luck and sometimes you create your own luck.

Business owners, executives and managers bear the risk and responsibility of a business. The responsibility of taking risks for some-one else (the owners of the business, employees etc) suggests a need for caution, unless mandates are clear that 'high risk' is acceptable. Align your personal risk profile with that of the business and the work at hand. The risk profile of the collective business defines the risk mood.

Gut feel comes from experience and experience comes from living mistakes

Managing risk

In order to manage risk you need to:

Identify what the risks are. There are risks all around us and we cannot always identify them. Your ability to spot potential risks improves with experience. Be open to information and really listen more than what you talk.

Predict when a risk might occur. There are normally signs that a risk is about to materialize or that the climate is trending towards risk. Some of the signs may be clear; others could be misleading. Often the signs are only identified after the risk has occurred. Your ability to predict risk also improves with experience. Research and identify systems that help you detect and predict risk.

Identify factors influencing the risk. Every risk is influenced by certain factors, some known and some hidden. Try and identify as many influencers as you can. Ideally, if you have any influence over any of these factors, this helps reducing risk.

Evaluate the identified risks. Study the various factors that could create and manifest risk and evaluate them. The more you understand them, the better you can manage them.

Constantly reassess the risk cycle. Experienced people constantly identify the risks, predict their occurrence and possible outcomes as well the factors which influence them. Understanding this risk cycle leads to successful risk management.

Keep the risk cycle always in view: spot it – see what could affect it – take steps to manage it – keep an eye on it.

Success is sweet; failure is bitter

What happens if I fail?

Potential outcomes of risk and failure include:

1. Financial losses. Just about every-thing in business is measured in financial terms. Money is a yard-stick. No-

body likes losing money, so failure through risk materializing is always going to incur direct and collateral damage. Even when risk and probabilities have been clearly pre-defined, the after-taste of losses is bitter.

2. Opportunity cost. Investing resources and time into a business, project, product, people etc is an 'investment' in so many ways. When risk results in failure, often there are lost opportunities and sometimes there are new opportunities. The new opportunities normally vest with others who are better positioned and they leverage your weaker position. The 'what-if' scenarios can hurt.

3. Reputational loss. A business, executive or manager who is associated with risk and losses will find his reputation and credibility suffering. Everything goes through cycles and there are cycles of luck. However, the good businesses, executives and managers overcome these challenges and they keep their reputation intact. Failure of any sort in our modern and materialistic society feeds gossip. Competitors, colleagues and the like may experience pleasure in your failure. It takes strong ones to rebuild after a 'hit'.

4. Temptation with dishonesty. In times of business difficulty, businesses, executives, managers and owners may be tempted into taking actions and making decisions they would ordinarily avoid. These actions are normally unethical, dishonest or plain illegal and they have a habit of being exposed, sooner or later. Real Leaders have faith and they honor universal principles.

5. Personal relationships suffer. Many personal relationships are damaged by failure. The stresses and pressures around a failing business, executive and manager and those around

him or her are sometimes too heavy to bear. These pressures tend to make people act 'out of character'. Look after relationships and marriages.

6. Recovery. It takes an investment of time, effort, training, counselling and money to recover from failure. The various financial, personal and psychological costs of recovering after a failure can be substantial.

Am I made of the 'the Right Stuff'?

Working for business as an owner, executive or manager isn't always an easy undertaking. It takes a special kind of person to make it successful and hopefully, pleasurable. Studies have shown that people with the following general personality characteristics normally stand a greater chance of being successful in business.

A successful owner, executive or manager;
- is goal driven
- has charisma
- can calculate and take risks
- is self-sufficient and self-supporting
- is credible and trustworthy
- is tenacious and doesn't give up
- is stubborn, but not at all costs
- can identify and leverage opportunity
- works 'smart' and economically
- is concise, gets to the point clearly
- delegates
- connects well with others
- motivates
- leads

- controls and manages well
- is quick thinking
- has a good memory
- is shrewd
- can handle stress
- is resilient, can take knocks
- is driven by success in all its forms
- is permanently enthusiastic and motivated
- is people orientated
- has composure, not easily flustered
- is sensitive to changing circumstances and environments
- can make a 'good' decision while not having all the information
- is sensitive to their 'gut feel'
- is intuitive
- has a high sense of personal pride
- is a creative thinker and worker
- is competitive
- puts the business first, before personal needs
- has high self-confidence
- not always forgiving of failure, their or others

There are always exceptions to any rule. People develop and improve their personalities and skills. However, if your personal characteristics substantially differ from those broad ones noted above, then you should consider some personal development before you get into business and attempt to be an owner, executive or manager.

Case study : A fishy story

A very risk tolerant entrepreneur started a fish farm business that cost millions to build and establish. Most of the funds were lent from Government as they were keen to fund these type of agricultural and food production projects. The business obviously needed a constant supply of quality fresh water, so the Government issued a Special Permit that allowed the business to be built alongside a large national river. Some of the rivers water flow was diverted into the fish farm where it provided the free natural resource for the fish to breed, grow and eventually be harvested.

Part of the Business Plan due diligence entailed analyzing historical Flood records for the region and the river and common 'expert' consensus was that flooding would be a low risk threat.

Year three of operations saw the worst floods in living memory and literally, every single fish in the fish farm was swept down the river, gone. It cost millions to re-stock and start from scratch again.

Chapter 3

Buy or Start Up

There are many motives for 'getting into business' and it is important to recognize what these motives are. The decision to start a business is probably one of the most important and far-reaching commitments you could make in a lifetime. Getting started entails an investment of personal effort, finances, sacrifices and risks. There are no guarantees of success but rewards can be very sweet.

Personal motivations

If your personal motives are unclear or not strong enough when getting into business, then you should consider delaying your decision until a later date. Do not commit yourself unless you have a strong conviction that you will succeed. Getting into business requires being strong. Half measures and poor commitment will lead to failure.

Businesses are normally capitalistic by nature as they aim to make a profit. If your business doesn't make a profit and it loses money, then that money is lost forever, gone. If you are going into business and you don't have an intense desire to make money and profits, then you need to think again. Be sure of your motives.

Personal reasons for wanting to get into business could include a combination of the following:

- to make money, or make more money
- to enjoy a new experience
- to stop working for a 'Boss'
- to be independent and to gain a sense of control of your life
- to prove your capabilities, often to yourself as much as to others
- for economic survival and to generate income
- to satisfy a need for change
- you could be in a personal or professional 'rut'
- to leverage an opportunity that has presented itself
- to create employment for family members

Buying an existing business

Many people consider buying an existing business rather than starting a new one. The apparent advantages and reasons for this choice may include some of the following:

Quicker access to markets
The business already engages with a market/s and there is an existing customer and supplier base.

Existing infrastructure
There are established systems, resources, procedures and ways of doing certain things.

Instant sales and income
An existing business is already trading and there is an existing turnover, cash flow and – hopefully – profit.

Management and staff
There will be an instant Management Team, hopefully a good one and then staff. This human resource is what determines business success or failure.

Less risk
Studies have shown that around 80% of all new businesses fail within five years, so purchasing an existing business suggests that risks are reduced.

Secure a trading position or an attractive lease
Finding viable sites and favorable leases is a difficult task, especially for retail businesses and those which require high pedestrian flows, street visibility, good parking. An existing business may hold 'value' in its real estate holdings.

Instant technology
An existing business may have technology, designs, business methods, systems or equipment which could be difficult to acquire or prohibitively expensive to reproduce.

Barriers to entry
Certain industries have barriers to entry that make it difficult for new entrants to get into the market. Purchasing an existing business would overcome this problem.

Reduce competition
By buying a competitor, one is actually reducing direct competition. This should lead to greater market share and profits.

Business synergy
Combining two or more businesses (new or existing) creates a powerful commercial synergy. Synergy can be achieved through improved profits, lower costs, more combined resources, broader product range, and greater rationalization.

Tax benefits
Some businesses hold tax benefits, usually in the form of assessed losses, which can be offset against future profits. For example, if

one business is extremely profitable and has high income tax payments it might be worthwhile buying a competitor business that has assessed losses. These assessed losses offer a tax and cash saving.

A quicker viable return on investment
An existing business usually offers immediate cash returns and start-ups have a start-up phase, usually characterized by losses.

Start up from scratch

Alternatively, the main advantages of starting a business from scratch can include:

No goodwill costs
Buying an existing business normally entails paying for goodwill in one form or another. Goodwill is basically the amount actually paid for a business, less the value of the physical assets that formed part of the sale. Starting your own business allows you to build up your own goodwill.

Cheaper
Goodwill costs aside, it may be cheaper in other ways. The new business may have better and cheaper business methods, technologies, systems and overhead structures may be significantly better.

No Bad will
You have Goodwill and you get Bad will. Purchasing an existing business includes inheriting that businesses history, both the good and the bad.

Choice and flexibility

Starting from new allows for greater choices and flexibility, as the business is not bound by any past history, existing structures or systems. Management can choose the size of the business, trading location, staff, trade names, business methods, customer policies and supplier choices. The business can grow without any past encumbrances.

Quicker

Finding a business that meets most of a new buyer's requirements can take a significant period of time. A new business may be quicker to start from new than to wait for an indefinite period of time trying to secure the right purchase.

Chapter 4

Legal

Often, business owners, executives or managers start a business or project without being fully compliant and legit. That is a sign of entrepreneurship.

Not being fully legal or compliant creates risk and this leads to 'exposure' and possibly costs and complications later on. Sometimes too, willfully not being compliant is a consequence of a defiant belief that formalizing your business 100 % just creates unnecessary costs. This is partially true, but the consequences of not being legal and complaint can cost you a lot more.

Identify what registrations are required for your business. Typically, these will include:

The legal name

Your business should be seen as a separate person or entity from you, the owner. The common forms of business ownership are a sole proprietor (sole trader), partnership and corporation / company (private or public).

Sole proprietor or sole trader

Typically, registration merely includes identifying the business as a sole proprietor / trader in the various business dealings and transactions the business has.

For example:

> 'Mr J Bloggs, trading as (doing business as) Bed Bug Eliminators'
> J Bloggs t/a (dba) Bed Bug Eliminators
>
> Bed Bug Eliminators
> Proprietor: J Blogs

Partnership

Typically, registration includes identifying the business as a partnership in the various business dealings and transactions the business has. These are common ownership choices for professional business people like attorneys, doctors, accountants, architects, engineers etc.

For example:

> J Bloggs, M Muggs and partners trading as (doing business as) Bed Bug Eliminators
> J Bloggs, M Muggs and partners t/a (dba) Bed Bug Eliminators
>
> Bed Bug Eliminators
> Partners: J Bloggs, M Muggs & partners

Corporations and Companies

Typically, registration entails registering the business with a government agency of sorts. A unique identity number is allocated to every entity formed and this identifies the business as legally registered.

For example:

> Investment Moves LLC
> EIN 452093583
> Document # L11000053721

The Trading name

The trading name of the business is the name that identifies the business to the general public, its suppliers and others. All businesses have a trade name but sometimes the trade name and the legal name are different

For example:

> Kill The Bug (trade name)
> Bed Bug Eliminators LLC (registered name)
> 95/06416/23 (registration number)

Identify your business

It is important that your business is well presented and readily identifiable. Customers and potential suppliers need to be aware of your business form, your management team, your registered names and trade names. The following methods of identification are generally accepted for the different business forms:

Company details could be printed onto the following:

- Brochures
- Business cards
- Check books
- Contracts and agreements
- Payroll documents
- Invoices and Bills
- Letterheads
- Letters of appointment
- Marketing materials
- Adverts
- Price lists
- Purchase orders
- Estimates
- Web pages

With whom do I register?

Every business will need to register with most of the following departments or bodies:

Tax authorities

- Register the business as an income taxpayer so that tax on profits, distributions and dividends are paid.
- Register the business as an employer of staff so that all employees pay tax and associated levies and insurances.
- Register for Sales Tax / Value Added Tax (VAT), as applicable.

- Register business owners, individually as taxpayers so that business owners pay tax on salaries, bonuses and profit distributions.

Corporation / Company registrar

- You need a Company Register for the corporation or company.
- The Company Register records information like shareholders, directors, auditors, addresses, registered names, type of equity issued,

Safety and Occupation

Businesses need to register, usually with government type authorities, so that the right contributions are paid to the right authorities which will entitle employees to benefits in times of injury or disablement incurred whilst in the workplace. Failure to do this places the business at risk as any injury incurred whilst in the work place could easily become a costly liability for the business, especially injuries and claims on a protracted nature. Costs generally include medical costs and payroll compensation.

Local government

Registering the business in instances where city and municipal laws apply, such as trading from home, flea market sites, food trucks, temporary licenses etc. Sometimes there are additional local business taxes to pay and additional may be required.

Union bodies

When employees belong to union or similar representative bodies, registering the business and its employees is required so that the correct levies are paid.

Liquor and regulatory boards

Some businesses need to be registered with certain regulatory boards so that some form of control and management is placed on the industry. Typical examples include businesses involved with liquor, second-hand goods, weapons, chemicals and medical equipment and supplies.

Design office

Registering a new product that may have certain new design characteristics which the business seeks to protect and preserve.

Patent office

Registering a brand-new and novel product that has commercial value which the business seeks to protect. Usually, the design has not been shared in the public domain and it must be a 'secret' before it qualifies for registering.

Trademark office

Registering a style of word, symbol or device that is unique to a business and its trading activities, which the business seeks to protect.

Business and Professional associations

Registering the business or business owners in their personal capacities with organized bodies or associations that represent the professions of the business owners or the business eg, Chamber of Commerce etc.

Getting registered

Each registration process and organization has its own unique set of rules and requirements. You may therefore consider appointing a professional such as an auditor, accountant, attorney, or business consultant to attend to the various registrations that are required and to maintain them.

Maintaining registrations

It is prudent if your appointed professional either maintains the registrations for the business or at least reviews on them on a regular basis. The various rules and laws applicable to each registration frequently change and you may not know or comply with the changes. The cost of incorrectly maintaining a registration can be quite substantial, especially those which have been mistakenly maintained for a long period of time. Leave it to the professionals.

One man's poison is another's bread

Getting caught

The responsibility of being registered with all the appropriate authorities, as well as fully complying with the relevant laws, vests with the business owners, executives or managers. Consult with your accountant, attorney, or professional adviser so that all required registrations can be identified and complied with.

However, business owners do sometimes fail to register with all or some of the authorities. They might even neglect records or fall behind on payments and dues, especially if the business is under hardship. Once this activity commences, matters quickly escalate and liabilities grow in terms of late payments, penalties and interest.

In many instances government bodies do share records. Example; what you declare on Sales Tax records for sales could be accessed by the Income Tax authorities when they review your income tax filings, so there is a cross-reference on Total Sales.

Should a liability for non-compliance ever materialize, a repayment plan can be negotiated with the relevant authorities. Rarely can any business afford to settle these large amounts in one or two payments. The authorities do wish to keep businesses trading employing staff and these authorities are open to honest negotiations regarding repayment plans.

The authorities are usually lenient enough not to press serious charges and take hard action, although they have the authority and means to do so.

Do not be tempted into falsifying your records in an attempt to reduce your payments and liabilities. Such actions are criminal and you have been warned.

Case Study: Pay the Taxman

A business selling certain products was owned by one person whose entrepreneurial personality pushed him to always take 'calculated' chances.

The business was required to submit monthly returns to substantiate sales tax records and payments. Every month, the owner under-declared the returns by around 10 % which he thought was inconsequential.

This practice went on for nearly ten years until one day Tax Officers arrived at the business and immediately confiscated documents, records and computer equipment as part of an audit. The data was all analyzed and the Tax Authorities recalculated all the undeclared taxes and added penalties and interest. The final adjusted account owing in back taxes was in the millions.

The owner initially tried to fight the tax audit but could-not deny the findings. He was lucky enough not be charged with Tax Fraud and the Tax Authorities approved a repayment plan and ultimately it took him nearly 8 years with monthly tax payments to repay this liability.

The Tax Authorities also secured their liability by attaching all his business and personal assets with Liens and there was a write-up about the business in the local newspapers, much to the delight of some competitors.

After everything had finally been repaid, the owner calculated that he had paid three times more than what he should have paid if he had been honest and compliant. He admitted to learning a hard lesson.

Chapter 5

Funding

The principal sources of finance are usually a combination of:

- Owners of the business
- Outside or third parties, such as banks or family members

The principal application of those funds is usually a combination of:

- Working capital, typically required for cash flow purposes.
- Capital expenditure (capex), typically required to purchase capital goods and assets such as equipment, vehicles and premises.

Typical questions that are asked when funding are:

- How much money is required?
- What are the funds for?
- How often will the funds be required (just once, or repeatedly like a credit line)?
- When and how will the funds be repaid?
- What are the costs of funding?
- What are the general terms and conditions?

Banks act like friends but they rarely help when you really need them

Applying for funds

When applying for funding you should consider the following factors:

How much money do you need?

It is important to establish how much funding is required in order to identify its likely source. You might be able to afford a relatively small amount yourself, while a larger investment may require funding from a third party such as a bank.

Determining how much money is required can only be done through intensive budget exercises such as cash flow forecasts, inventory calculations, estimating production cycles, determining project start-up costs and basically identifying all the costs that will be incurred over a given time.

It is advisable to slightly overestimate the amount required, as in most cases the best plans and budgets are too conservative. Rather lend too much and repay the surplus than start with too little. Not having enough funding puts the whole business / project at risk. Going back to lenders asking for more funding at a later date gives a poor impression. Rarely do projects complete under Budget, they are mostly completed being over Budget.

How often will you need it?

Working capital / cash flow needs often fluctuate over time. The business / project might require an open credit line facility, where you have a set amount / limit of funds available from which you can draw and repay as and when it suits your cash flow needs. This type of funding is similar to traditional overdraft facilities. Working capital type funding is considered short term funding as typically these are repaid in a short term, less than 3 years.

Usually with large Capital expenditures for assets like equipment and vehicles, funding is required each time there is a purchase. The purchase may involve purchasing one or more capex items at a time. Capital items are usually funded using medium to long term finance, typically repayable in steady monthly or interval instalments over 3 to 5 years.

When building real estate, funds are sometimes split into two types of funds. One for the building project activity where there are no capital repayments and loan interest is capitalized and a second when the building is completed and a repayment activity commences. Whilst the building is being erected and built and funds are normally released in progress draws with inspections each time a draw is requested. If completed real estate is being purchased, the funds are paid out upon closing or transfer. Funding for real estate is usually long term, for commercial and business type real estate the term is usually 10 to 15 years and for residential real estate it is usually 15 to 30 years, with 20 years being the most common term.

Sometimes funding can be a mix of short-term working capital and medium to long term capex and real estate funding. Attempt to secure funding that suits your needs. You have to match the funding term with the asset type and generally opt for a longer repayment term than a shorter repayment term, as this reduces the value instalment amount, so making it easier to meet every month. One can always accelerate or increase payments if there is surplus cash / profits. If you short-pay on an instalment or miss instalments, lenders panic and this will affect your credit rating and cause problems.

How long will you need the money for?

Lenders need to know how long you anticipate needing funds.

Working capital

- It might be just for a couple of days whilst you wait for certain receivables to be collected and come into the business.
- Cash credit lines and Overdrafts are usually approved for periods of up to a year, but are usually renewable. Credit lines and Overdrafts can also be withdrawn with little or no notice and this can cause problems.
- If a loan for working capital is taken, these are usually repayable up to a period of three years. These loans are usually taken to fund expansions, the purchase of base stock and so on and not to assist with typical weekly and monthly cash flow cycles.

Capex / Assets

- Loans for computer equipment and systems are usually repayable within three years, coinciding with the commonly accepted period of depreciation / accounting write-off for this kind of equipment
- Loans for the purchase of manufacturing equipment and including vehicles are usually repaid within three to five years, as this also coincides with the depreciation / accounting write-off periods applicable to this type of asset.
- Loans for the purchase of real estate are usually repaid within ten to twenty years.

When will you be making repayments?

Establish when the funds are repayable so that you can budget for them. Loans can usually be repaid in equal installments monthly or quarterly over a number of years. Credit lines and overdrafts are usually renewable annually but can also be repayable on demand, with little to no notice.

Also inquire if loans can be repaid sooner as often there are penalty clauses in the loan agreements where earlier or accelerated repayments are not allowed or else they attract extra interest or costs. A common example is that vehicles are often sold or replaced before whilst they still have a loan balance due on them. The lender allows the loan to be repaid in full but will often raise a 90-day penalty interest charge for the early settlement of the loan.

Be aware of all likely costs

Securing funds will create various costs. Typically these could include administration fees, valuation fees, loan raising fees, bond registration costs, title fees, title insurance costs, legal costs, stamp duties etc. Clarify and identify what costs are applicable to the transaction to avoid surprises and so that you can budget for them accurately. Usually these costs are not clearly established or explained in the early stages of a funding discussion and only after a huge amount of time and effort has been invested in the transaction do the facts become clear and one can feel a little 'ambushed'.

Determine interest rates and similar costs

Moneylenders are in the business of making a profit from lending money. This profit is usually in the traditional form of an interest rate. However, there are other forms of return that a moneylender may seek. These could include a share of profits, a percentage of sales, the issue of free or cheap shares, receiving dividends, or buying or being granted certain benefits from the business such as discounted products. Clarify exactly what borrowing money is going to cost you.

Other conditions

Sometimes other terms and conditions can apply when you are borrowing money and these can include the lender requiring life assurance policies from key owners and managers, nominating one of their directors onto your board, needing regular copies of management accounts and financial reports, having regular site visits to the business, preventing the repayment of any funds / loan accounts to owners until such time that debt / equity ratios are achieved and having obscure loan clauses that give the lender title to your accounts receivable assets.

Some of these terms and conditions could have potentially far-reaching consequences for your business, so always be cautious and do-not agree or sign documents without fully understanding them.

Expect the unexpected

Is security required?

In order to protect their investment, moneylenders typically require security to safeguard and hedge any risk they are taking by lending the money. In practice, these securities give the lender legal rights to take ownership and possession of business and personal assets. The lender can then sell these assets in order to recover his lost funds.

Typical securities that may be made available to a lender include:

- Title or bonds over business or residential premises (immovable property).

- Title or bonds over plant, equipment and similar assets (moveable property).
- Cessions over monetary investments like fixed deposit and cash accounts.
- Cessions over investment policies that have cash value.
- Cessions over life assurance and endowment policies that have cash value.
- Cession over equity / shares, preferably shares in publicly listed companies / corporations rather than private companies.
- Credit or lease agreements over plant, equipment or vehicles (capital goods) financed by the moneylender (basically, the lender owns the asset until it is paid for in full; then ownership passes to the borrower).
- Cession over any monies invested in the business by the business owners ie their Loan Accounts.
- Cession over monies owed to the business by Debtors, Staff Loans and the like.
- Personal sureties or guarantees by the business owners, key managers, directors or third parties.
- Sureties or guarantees from other businesses.
- Cession, pledges, or hypothecates over anything of reasonable value, such as patents, royalty agreements and contracts.

You may feel that moneylenders generally place a low valuation value on the various assets that may be offered as security. For example, a bank may value a residential property 20% less than its reasonable market value; publically listed shares may be valued at 50% of current trading prices. The reason for this is that when circumstances force a moneylender to act on any security there are normally additional costs, such as outstanding monthly loan repayments or interest payments that need to be covered. Further, when selling recovered assets the moneylenders are hasty and they don't always get a reasonable selling price for the assets they have recovered.

Formal moneylenders are extremely cautious and they safeguard their interests and budget for a 'worst case scenario'. They will always seek to be over-secured in a way, but they will deny this.

Renegotiating loan agreements

Businesses do not always trade well or according to plan and sometimes agreements need to be renegotiated. If possible, establish the lender's policies in case of this eventuality. If your business runs into financial problems it may require financial refinancing and restructuring including capitalization of interest, or a moratorium (postponement) on repayments.

Some moneylenders may have a 'hard line' policy and immediately force the repayment of loans and others might be more willing to assist. However, assistance is normally only given if the moneylender is certain that your business will survive its current problems and that there is no risk involved. Certain laws also prevent overly creative financing structures.

What do I need for a loan application?

Documentation

Moneylenders need documentation to analyze and process. Firstly, before you submit any application you need to establish what documentation the lender requires. Typically, this might include:

- *Business application forms, lender templates.* These normally request legal and general information on the business and details of the funding required.

- *Personal application forms, lender templates.* These request personal information on the business owners or directors, together with details as to what personal assets and liabilities they may have.
- *Business plan.* This can be either a concise or a lengthy document, depending on the amount required and the complexity of the transaction. Basically, you should attempt to advise the lender of the general activities of the business. The lender is looking for some 'comfort' that your business is 'solid' and worthy of funding.
- *Motivation for funding.* This details the need for funding and could include cash flow projections, budgets and supporting documents like estimates for capital purchase and calculations supporting new inventory requirements and working capital needs. The moneylender needs to ascertain and test how much, why, and when the funding is going to be repaid.
- *Legal documentation.* Typically, copies of the business's registration and formation forms (articles and memorandums, partnership agreements, etc.) will be asked for, together with director / owner identity documents. Other documentation may include ownership documents for any assets being tendered as security- such as deeds and title for real estate, original stock certificates, vehicle titles etc.
- *Financial information.* Businesses that have a trading history will be required to submit copies of the past years' annual financial statements and income tax filings, as well as cash flow forecasts, sales forecasts, overhead expenses, breakeven analyses, project workings and a SWOT analysis.
- *Other supporting documentation.* Certain additional documentation may be necessary, such as estimates for

intended asset purchases, signed deed of sale for any real estate being purchased, valuation reports and so on.

Policies

Moneylenders have different policies. Some don't offer certain types of funding, while others only specialize in particular financing. There may be minimum and maximum amounts. You may find that certain lenders don't fund small businesses at all. Some lending companies may not fund goodwill when buying a business or research and development costs. Some lenders may have a strict ethical policy and won't fund any company that trades in industries perceived to be immoral.

In general, lenders are only going to consider loan applications that meet and comply with their own lending policies. Don't waste your time by applying for funding with lenders that are not taking you seriously.

Quality of business management

Lenders place great importance on the quality of management that run the business. This lender policy supports the basic belief that a well-managed business has a higher chance of survival. Poor management usually leads to business failure.

Lenders will acquire and assess information on the management team. This may include a visit the business and meetings with key management staff. Lenders will evaluate education levels, earning potential, reputations, personal net worth, Resumes and the like.

The quality of the submitted business plan and supporting documentation also creates an important perception with regard to the quality of the management. If the submitted business plan is unprofessional, full of mistakes and doesn't make any sense, this creates a poor impression and won't enable a successful loan transaction.

Matching the funding

All funds must be correctly matched and utilized. A sound financial principle is that:

- Real estate should be financed using long-term debt (10- to 20- year repayment period).
- Capital items, such as vehicles, plant and equipment should be funded using medium term debt (3- to 5- year repayment period).
- Working capital should be financed using short-term debt (up to 3 years).

Ensure that your funding needs are correctly matched with the right type of funding. Lenders will rarely fund the purchase of business real estate a three-year loan as the monthly installments would be so high that the borrower would not be able to afford it. By the same token, you are also unlikely to find a funding for a vehicle purchase with a 10 year loan.

Profitability of the business

A business can only repay loans and pay interest if it makes a reasonable profit. Lenders will assess the historical profitability of a business, as well as its predicted profitability. This is achieved through an analysis of historical financial statements and other data. Lenders usually have their own financial models that they use in an assessment such as this.

Many small businesses fail these tests because their financial statements and records are usually outdated, inaccurate, incomplete and under-stated. Very few small businesses have annual financial statements that indicate reasonable or high level of profitability.

Lenders are strongly guided by past profit history and not future predictions.

Viability of the funding need

Lenders need to hear the benefits of an expansion within the business. Lenders want to see progress, savings, bigger profits, productivity, near ideas and positivity.

A lender may believe that the same outcome could be achieved in another way. For example, you might wish to purchase your own business real estate but your lender might feel it is better to continue leasing. You need to present viable, business-orientated reasons. If your need for finance is poorly motivated, or appears unviable, you will have a problem securing funds.

Free lunches are myth

Security

Moneylenders need security. The more the better. Without security the chances of borrowing money are poor. The greater the amount required, the better quality and higher value of security will be required.

Ask the moneylenders to show how they calculate and determine the security ratio or percentage for the loan. From this information you will see how certain security values are calculated: for example, a residence may be valued at 20% below market value; publicly listed stocks may be valued at 50% of current market value, accounts receivables may only be valued at 30% of value. Equipment and vehicles may only be valued at between 20 % and 50 % of value.

Credit-worthiness

How have other loans and debts been managed? A potential lender will use information from credit bureaus and credit informational systems in order to evaluate how you or your business has managed previous loans and debts.

Banking systems are integrated. Banks assist one another with information on how accounts are managed. Credit bureaus collect public court records that can indicate a history of insolvencies, liquidations, and credit judgments. These are taken in a poor light. Other information is also collected from suppliers, landlords and others who may advise that you or your business is a slow or bad payer.

Owners and key managers are also personally reviewed and analyzed. If any have poor credit scores, insolvencies and the like, this may contaminate the business or project.

Overall, any information indicating a poor credit-worthiness will pose a problem.

Case study : Murphy's Golden Rule: 'The man with the gold makes the rules'

A business developed a new and exciting product that stood to make a lot of money if it could get to market. The business owners just didn't have the funds required to leverage this opportunity, so they put together a business plan and started looking for investors. First they tried family and friends but these didn't have spare money and/or desire to invest. Then they tried the banks but the banks needed so much loan security which the owners didn't have.

Eventually the owners found a private investor. However, the investor wanted significant equity / shares in the business as well as a large share of the profits.

The business owners now faced a dilemma. Were they to abandon the new product and continue on as they had in the past, or were they to accept the fact that investors generally demanded a lot of 'return' for their investment.

After deliberating, the business owners accepted 'Murphy's Golden Rule' and accepted the investors offer and together they made a lot of money. Even more than what the owners had made before they developed this new product. The business owners now realized that although they had less equity percentage in the business, the equity 'value' was significantly higher as the business had grown so much with the new product and the funding it had secured.

Chapter 6

A Basic Business Plan

Why have a business plan?

'Planning' increases your chances of a successful outcome. All owners, executives or managers should have a business plan and a plan for themselves within this business plan. The more comprehensive and considered it is, the higher the chances that the plan will work. Plans do not always need to be strictly adhered to, but they are vital if you are to give yourself and / or the business direction and goals. A plan should tell you what you want to achieve, when you want to achieve it and how you will achieve it. The plan should be internalized so that it becomes part of the daily consciousness and so that all work orientates around this plan.

A business plan details exactly how a business will be established and run. It considers all material aspects of the business; such as the form of ownership, the proposed trading activities, management duties and responsibilities, the marketing plan, the production plan, the human resources plan, and the financial plan. It will be a relatively lengthy document and may take some time to put together. It's worth the investment.

Preparing a business plan is a critical step towards running a successful business and project. Many a business or project has failed due to a lack of planning or because the plan was of poor quality. And once the plan is in place, you must _use_ it. Plans are often made but not followed enough.

Good plans should be as objective as possible. They should be reviewed by a wide range of experienced people. Inputs and contributions should be welcomed from all sides. Often, contributions from a third party highlight critical flaws or important issues that were overlooked or not considered by the person/s formulating the business plan. Consider as many of the permutations as possible.

Well-prepared business plans force objectivity and reality on the owners, executives and managers for the benefit of the business or project. Owners, executives and managers should constantly review and compare actual results achieved with those originally forecasted. Establish where there are variances between the plan and reality exist and try to determine why the variance gap occurred. Corrective steps and measures can then be taken to prevent a recurrence of the same problem.

Look before you leap

What is the purpose of the plan?

A business plan is normally used as a planning tool when going into business or starting a new project like an expansion, a new division or new product line. It should be a well-presented written document in which all the material facts and issues relating to the business and its environment are documented. The length of the business plan varies depending on the size and complexity of the project and the purpose of the plan itself.

Third parties, such as banks, money lenders, landlords, suppliers and government bodies frequently request business plans in order to gain an understanding and assessment of the a business or project.

Often it is necessary to change the style and presentation of the business plan and its contents in order to suit the audience using the business plan.

Ultimately, design and create the plan so that the plan users will easily understand it. Once understood, it becomes easier to follow.

When in doubt, leave it out

Proposed layout

There are many permutations to preparing a business plan and it could be presented along the following lines:

- Name of the business or project.
- Contact details or person/s responsible for the business plan and author acknowledgments.
- Table of contents. This breaks the plan down into logically separate sections, each clearly defined.
- An introduction. This describes why the business plan was prepared and what the business aims to achieve. It should also include a brief background on the nature of the business or project.
- Date stamp. The business plan should be dated so that users know when the business plan was completed and presented.

Topics covered should be grouped into separate sections and could include the following:

- Form of business ownership

- Company structure
- Management and staffing structure
- Product and service lines, sales and marketing
- Competition and positioning
- Manufacturing and production
- Supply chain, purchasing, quality and logistics
- Finance, breakeven analysis, analytics and administration
- SWOT analysis
- Annexures

How big will my business or project be?

It is important to have some early thoughts about where you see your business or project going. Consider the following:

- The estimated size of the business or project.
- An estimate of the $-value finances required for investment in the business or project.
- The products or services offered.
- The estimated selling prices and costs of the product or service offered.
- The estimated break-even point and sensitivity analysis.
- The estimated manpower needs.
- The required equipment and asset needs.
- The number of owners to be involved.
- An estimated starting date for the business or project.

Taking this information as a starting point, one needs to 'size' the business and project first of all. This is important because it determines the direction and path taken in preparing the plan. If the business or project is relatively small and simple, then obviously the business plan will be small and simple. If the business or project is going to big, then the business plan will be big.

Don't just start on a plan without first sizing the business or project, as you may quickly realize that you have begun on the wrong path and you have wasted time and not considered what you should have.

Before you start anything - The basic calculations – Break-even point and sensitivity analysis

For any business or project there are always a few critical issues that will define the business or project.

Every business or project has a 'break-even' point. This is the critical point which defines whether the business or project will achieve the financial and / or through-put volumes required to succeed, or fail.

It is critical that the break-even point be established and that the break-even point be fair and realistic. Do-not under-estimate the break-even point or manipulate it to make the business or project appear viable, in theory. Many a business plan has been manipulated so that it reads well but reality is what counts at the end of the day.

Estimate overheads, especially big costs like Payroll which normally also determine capacities. Be conservative with Gross Profit Margins (GP's) and allow for erosion due to discounts, competitive pricing etc. Once Overheads are determined, do some sensitivity analysis using 'best case' and 'worst case' Gross Profit Margins, unit selling prices, capacities etc. All of this analysis and elasticity testing will assist in conceptualizing the business or project and near correctly sizing it. Critical flaws are also more likely to be revealed and you will begin to understand what resources are required, what are capacity constraints, staffing requirements, trading hours required, production times required, market share required, comparisons with competitors, material supplies etc. A lot of things start falling into place once you can visualize your break-even points.

Adhering to the following proposed format, you now need to gather information and make certain important decisions.

What form of ownership do I need?

When making your decision you must consider the following points:

How much investment do I need? A greater amount of money invested in a business generally implies a higher level of formality. More owners are likely to be involved and the level of control and reporting will be similarly increased.

How quickly do I want to get started? Generally, a sole trader / proprietor is the quickest business form to set up. However, certain accountants and attorneys offer pre-registered 'shelf' entities that can be used to speed up the time of getting into a formal business. These pre-registered entities typically require amendments to change their name/s and to reflect who the shareholders, officers and directors are. Other factors are capital requirements as some entities have government regulated capital requirements, the financial year-end (normally the official tax year is chose as this avoids having to complete additional accounting work etc).

Are start-up costs a problem? Formal entities like public companies are generally the most expensive business form to register and maintain and professional inputs are required for accounting and legal compliance. A sole proprietor is generally the cheapest, followed by a partnership and then variations in legal entities.

What are the tax implications? Each business form has various tax implications and it is recommended that an accountant be consulted for advice. It is important to get leverage the early losses that most businesses incur. Sometimes a tax loss made in say Year 1 cannot be rolled-over and leveraged in Year 2. Sometimes losses made in a sole trader / proprietor ownership structure cannot be rolled forward into the following year. Tax losses typically have a cash-value between 25 % and 40 % depending on applicable tax rates and circumstances eg. If the business makes a loss of $ 100,000 in Year One and then a Profit of $ 100,000 in Year Two, the Tax 'Cost' is probably Zero for both years. However, if the Profit in Year Two is $ 200,000, the Tax Cost is probably around $ 30,000 for both years. Tax losses that can be leveraged have a Market Cash Value.

How many owners are there in my business? The more owners and investors a business requires or has, the more formal and complex the ownership structure becomes. There are several agreements that are required to regulate matters between all the parties associated with the business and matters generally start getting more complicated. Legal advice is required and negotiations may be get tougher, as will reaching consensus. Minority Shareholders sometimes have a larger influence on matters compared to their respective Shareholding percentage.

Does my business have a special name? A business can have a legal name and a different second name, the trade name. However, preferably the two names should be the same. When registering

URL / web names, trade-marks etc, one should try get all these consistent and synchronized. Sometimes businesses wish to have similar names to much larger competitors but most often, not.

What is my professional image? Generally a sole trader / proprietorship and, to a lesser extent, common partnerships (not professional partners like lawyers, doctors and accountants) are seen to hold a low professional image in business. Sole traders and partnerships are considered to be 'informal'. The legally registered and regulated entities like companies and corporations are generally preferred in business by institutional businesses like bankers, suppliers etc as they require a higher degree of compliance.

Are third parties involved? Third parties may only lend, invest and transact with certain business forms. This is normally the case when the third party requires the business to hold high compliance standards so that accounting standards are high, there are external audits and high standards. This is often the case in dealings with foreign companies and their subsidies, transacting with government organizations and financial institutions that are investing or lending.

What is an effective business structure?

Businesses are usually divided and structured into various divisions or departments, each identified by its own group of unique work functions. It makes sense to group similar work activities together.

Depending on the size of the business, it may be necessary to overlap and combine certain departments. For example: finance and administration; marketing and sales; production; purchases, quality and logistics.

Bigger businesses may require structures that are more complex. This might mean dividing work and resources into divisions. Projects may also overlap and require input from common departments and this may become a matrix.
Sometimes a big business may create Projects / Divisions / Branches that are a small, reasonably independent business of sorts as they have their own divisions and departments but they still report to the bigger business.

As businesses grow and as things change, so does the structure of business. Often, analyzing bigger competitors and their evolution may assist in designing the most effective and lean structure for your business and division.

Issues to consider include when designing and choosing a structure may include;

- Need for flexibility,
- Cost sharing,
- Common or unique work processes,
- Work output - Manpower versus Automation,
- Products or Services,
- Type of work – Batch or Continuous,
- Physical space needed,
- Management skills and Span of Control,
- Degree of Management autonomy,
- Lines of communication,
- Geographical reach and markets,
- Logistics (supply and delivery),

Fig 1: Typical business activities

Department:	Finance	Administration	Marketing	Sales	Production	Purchases	Quality	Logistics
Functions:	Accounting records	Assisting other departments	Advertising	Discount management	Balancing production flows	Consumables	Analyse defects	Archiving records
	Annual financial statements	Employee records	After-sales service	Maintaining records	Bottlenecks	Costings	Certification	Maintaining records
	Banking	Faxes	Call centres	Merchandising	Capacities	Delivery costs	Collect & analyse statistics	Maintenance & repairs
	Business agreements	Filing	Competitor Analysis	Receiving sales orders	Data analysis	Discounts taken	Correct quality deviations	Security
	Cashflow planning	Internal mail (memos, etc.)	Guarantee policies	Sales budgets/forecasts	Down time	Duties & surcharges	Defective goods	Services
	Collecting from debtors	Mail	Maintaining records	Sales strategies	Efficiencies	Economic quantities	Inspections	Staff facilities
	Computer systems	Maintaining records	Market analysis	Samples to customers	Equipment choices	Foreign exchange	Maintaining records	Transportation
	Control systems	Meetings	Market research	Seeing customers	Handling	Guarantees	Markings	
	Costings	Office supplies	New products	Selling	Inspections	Imports	Measure quality	
	Credit policies	Personnel files & records	Pricing	Tele-sales	Jobs or batches	Maintaining records	Quality audits	
	Customer credit limits	Reception	Product launches		Layout	Packaging	Quality manuals	
	Fixed asset register	Switchboard	Public relations		Lead times	Raw materials	Quality policies	
	Insurance policies review	Typing	Seeing customers		Maintaining records	Signing delivery notes	Quality standards	
	Labour union relations	Writing cheques	Showroom		Materials	Stock control	Test reports	
	Legal issues		Training		Minimum runs	Stock -takes	Work instructions	
	Maintaining records		Website		Outputs	Stock turnover		
	Management reports				Planning & scheduling	Storage & facilities		
	Office equipment				Processes	Sub-assemblies		
	Paying creditors				Rejects and wastage	Supplier meetings		
	Payroll				Sales targets	Supplier records		
	Petty cash				Services required	Supplying production		
	Policies, procedures & rules				Systems	Tracking orders & deliveries		
	Preparing VAT returns				Tools required	Processing orders		
	Reconciliations				Work stations			
	Salary/wage structures							
	Staff issues							
	Statutory returns							
	Tax planning							
	Writing business plans							

How should I structure my staff?

Once you have determined a business structure it becomes easier to explore what staffing and management needs are required for your business and the functional departments. Each division and department will have certain functions and obviously people are required to fulfill these functions and manage work and people within that department.

The function of each department needs to be analyzed and documented so that enough duties can be grouped together to form sufficient work activity for a single person. The various functions that are grouped together result in a 'job description'.

Job description

This lists the tasks and activities to be performed, the responsibilities and the authorities and the reporting lines back to managers or the owners. It could also include information such as the job grade (what salary, level of authority and responsibility goes with that position). Job grades could be classified from Grade 1 to Grade 10. Additional information might include working hours, work benefits and other benefits.

Having compiled a job description, one can then document the critical and preferred skills a person will require in order to perform the tasks effectively and efficiently. This information is called a job specification, and it details and specifies the requirements for the person performing that particular job function. This could include the expected education level, required skills, relevant experience and ideal or suitable personality.

Recruiting staff

Once you have documented the job description and a job specification, recruiting staff is easier as it becomes clearer what staff you require. Applicants for positions offered by the business should submit Resumes with supplementary information. Information supplied by applicants should be verified and references are critical. Applicants can be given small tests applicable to their job description. Background checks are also recommended and these typically investigate criminal records and credit worthiness. Permission is typically required from the job applicants to perform background checks. Background checks should ideally be on-going and not a one-off 'snap-shot' as things change with time.

Employing the 'wrong' person can cost a business in many ways. Labor laws generally favor employees, so staff recruitment and hiring should always be done thoroughly and carefully. Probationary periods are recommended so that bad hiring choices can be corrected without much recourse.

Sales and marketing

One should by now have a good idea of the type of products or services being sold or what activities are going to be at the core of the project or business. By doing a business plan you may find that your original thoughts and ideas have changed a little, particularly as information on products, services and competitors is found and understood.

Decide what products or services your business will sell and specify them individually and, where possibly, into groups. Groups of similar products are called a product family and the collection of various products sold by the business is called a product range.

You need to have a well-balanced product family and well-balanced product range. A narrow product family or family range increases risks and limits sales; at the same time, too broad a product family or product range can increase costs without leveraging sales.

New products usually fail

It is important that you identify who will buy your products or services. These buyers are your potential customers. Customers often have similar characteristics:

- They trade in similar business sectors or industries.
- They have similar needs and wants.
- They may be in a certain geographical area.
- They have similar income profiles.
- They may be of similar ages.

By studying potential customers you will see that they can usually be grouped into separate categories. These are called target markets. Each target market is different and you should know these differences. By knowing and understanding the customer, you will begin to understand that makes him or her buy products or services.

A customer's purchase decision can be influenced by factors such as:

- the total experience the customer has when transacting with your business
- referrals and reviews
- staff – skills, product knowledge, appearance,
- price points
- quality standards and consistency
- availability of inventory
- product ranges and choices
- service levels
- infrastructure, safety and hygiene
- payment options (cash, card, credit terms, coupons etc)
- the strength of your differentiators and those of your competitors
- loyalty with other competitors or brand names
- displacement – something has forced the customer to try you
- location and accessibility
- delivery policies
- guaranty and return policies
- advertising and promotion appeal
- your time in business
- association - if a lot of Customers dislike the word Barack, naming a new product 'Barack' is not a clever name choice, no matter how good the product is. Conversely, you might just have really 'cool' advertisements and these are what attracts Customers to your 'average' products.

Know the competition

Competitors are normally already in business and they are already selling and working in the market/s you are choosing to join or that you already work in. Competitors do things in certain ways for certain reasons. Do-not under-estimate them and most importantly, learn from them but do-not become obsessed with them.

Analyze competitors and use your findings in your business plans and strategies. Whether competitors are large or small, you should be concerned with all competitors who are performing better than you, those that are growing and those who are shrinking. Rank yourself compared to your competitors and strive to be better, not necessarily bigger. A better business will eventually get bigger too.

Typically, direct head-to-head competition with competitors is unwise. Do-not focus on the competition, rather focus on the market and leverage the various differentiators you have over competition. Realistically, if you don't have any strong differentiators, then you need to get some fast.

A lot of businesses focus on competing against competition and this is not good strategy. Be open yet careful with competitors and try as hard as you can to stop them from learning what you are doing and what you are up to.

Competitors that are shrinking need to be understood and the reasons for their decline need to be identified. If your business has similar characteristics, this is a risky position and you may need to change.

Always remember, the market is bigger than all the competitors and the market holds the money, not your competitors.

When analyzing competitors you should look for and gather information such as:

- What is their financial position?
- How much money is invested in their business?

- Who are their owners?
- What special skills do their owners and managers have?
- How many staff do they employ?
- What staff turnover level do they have?
- How many customers do they have?
- Who are the largest customers?
- Where are their customers and why are they there?
- How do they 'look after' their customers?
- Why do their customers support them?
- What is their product range?
- Have their product ranges changed at all?
- If there are product changes, why?
- Which products sell best?
- Who are their suppliers?
- Do you have common suppliers?
- How much inventory do they carry?
- How much advertising do they do?
- How big are their premises?
- How long have they been in business?
- Have they grown or shrunk in the last few years and why?
- Have they purchased or sold any big ticket items lately?
- What is their break-even point?
- What are their weaknesses?
- What are their strengths?
- What are their main differentiators?
- What future plans do they have?
- What influence do they hold over the market?
- Do they have any special connections or relationships with other competitors?
- Do they have any special connections or relationships with key suppliers?
- Are there any formal or informal industry groupings who regulate the market in any way (collusion)?

Every factual and reasonably accurate piece of information about your competitors should be written down, studied and filed. Over a period of time these Competitor files will become an important source of business intelligence. Accurate and updated information on competitors can be priceless. This is business intelligence.

Be cautious with sharing information with your suppliers as they can be an information gateway to your competitors. There is usually some-one close to your business who shares your 'classified' information in the market-place to your detriment. Confidentiality Agreements with Employees and Suppliers set the tone a little but enforcing these Agreements is not always practical or possible.

Markets change, when will yours change?

Pricing policy

Pricing a product entails striking a balance between giving the product the best chance of being sold while at the same time giving your business an acceptable gross profit percentage. What a product costs and what it sells for are related issues but they are not directly linked.

When pricing your product you should consider the following points:

- What choices does the customer have? Generally, the less choice a customer has, the better the price that can be asked. This is simple Supply and Demand economics.

- Are there similar or competitive products? The more competition there is, the lower the prices will be and Over Supply can be a risk
- What price will the customer accept? Sometimes customers are willing or only able to pay a certain price, irrespective of the product benefits or other positive aspects.
- Will discounts be required? Discounts lower the pricing points and gross margins and profits.
- What direct and indirect costs relate to the sale? Direct costs include the cost of the actual product. Indirect costs include all the additional costs such as after-sales service, installation costs, telephone support, exchange and return rates and so on. If a product has indirect costs, then a higher sell price should be targeted in order to offset future indirect expenses that may be incurred in the complete sale cycle.
- The type of products to be sold. Certain products have regulated prices. These regulations may be prescribed by law or by the industry eg petroleum, metals, and precious stones.
- The sales mix. This is the range, or mix, of all products sold by the business. A business may choose to have a 'loss leader', which is a product sold at a very low price or even at cost. These loss leaders are used to attract customer attention through 'displacement' and hopefully entice new customers to the business. The strategy is that these new customers will also buy other products that carry better margins and that they will return and reward the business with future loyalty.
- Competitors' prices. Use competitors' prices as a guideline. You may wish to undercut, match or even exceed your competitors' prices. Be careful if your products are priced higher than those of your competitors and you cannot reasonably justify the higher prices with additional value or

benefits. Customers are not stupid and they need to understand why prices between competitors for the same / similar products differ substantially. Telling them why creates trust.

- End-user or not? Will your customers be selling the product on? Customers will want to add 'mark- up' to your price when they re-sell it. You must take these additions into account.
- Volatile price movements. If possible, avoid frequent changes to your prices. This can be done by forecasting and predicting future prices or holding your prices until you are forced to change them. Certain products such as those imported are influenced by foreign exchange fluctuations, or those whose input costs vary frequently (e.g. crude oil), have prices that change frequently.
- Gross profit. Ultimately, gross profit margins are the goal but you need first sell the product before you realize gross profit!
- Market resistance. It is easier reducing prices than increasing them. Going to customers with new and higher prices is not always well received and this creates distrust. Price increases create 'displacement' and this can easily prompt customers to look around and consider your competitors. Competitors can leverage your displacement and attempt to 'steal' your customers. Where possible, price increases should be implemented shortly after your larger competitors have price increases. Always try give some reasonable notice that prices are going to change.

Distribution

Typically, a distribution channel for a product is as follows:

1. *Raw product:* these are the basic goods used in the product. These are sold by producers to the manufacturers.
2. *Manufacturer(s):* these could be one or several who convert the raw materials into a finished or near finished products and who add 'value' to them through material inputs, labor inputs and creativity / intellectual property.
3. *Wholesaler:* they typically purchase from manufacturers and they re-sell products to resellers without any additional 'value', other than possibly linking / bundling the product with others and playing with discounts / pricing.
4. *Resellers / Retailers:* they purchase from wholesalers and then re-sell to the end users.
5. *The end user:* usually the general public, other businesses that are final users and consumers.
6. *The recycler:* unwanted products and waste are either dumped or sold. These can be recovered, reconverted and re-used; or they may be destroyed and left to degrade over time.

The **end user** is the most important customer. Without him or her there is no demand and therefore no sales chain. If the re-seller has no customers, then the wholesaler will have no customers and the manufacturer will have no customers.

Every business that handles a product through-out the sale cycle needs to make a profit on the transaction. This means that the more a product is handled and the longer the sales chain, the more cost goes into the product and the higher the selling price will be at the end of the sales chain.

One needs to determine and establish a distribution channel for the products being sold. Your choice of distribution channel will have a huge influence on your costings, marketing strategies and inventories.

How products will physically get to a customer is another a vital consideration in any business.

Marketing strategy

In drawing up a marketing strategy you should plan and detail what must be achieved, when it must be achieved and how it will be achieved. When you know what influences your customers' decision to buy products, then you are in a position to formulate a marketing strategy for your business. Within this strategy you need to attempt to meet as many of your customers' needs and requirements as possible – with the least cost and disruption to your own business.

By analyzing your competitors you will get an idea of what marketing strategies are probably best in the market you are all competing in. You might see new opportunities where you can make your own unique strategies perhaps better or more effective than competitors. Leverage your differentiators.

Your marketing strategy should be reviewed on a regular basis and tweaked, as required. Customers change, markets change, advertising mediums change, costs change and you need to evolve and change with these.

Sales budgets

Having done some basic business calculations, you will know what your break-even point / range is and the elasticity's around this. Similarly, having analyzed the competition, you will have an idea of what sales budgets are realistic. You need some benchmarks from which to make decisions and start formulating sales budgets and income streams.

Sales and income budgets should reflect the quantity and sales value of the products being sold. For example, 2000 units sold at $20 each totals $40,000 of gross sales.

Don't base your budges on what you wild like to achieve but rather aim for what is realistic. Your sales budgets also need to take into account the resources available such as the number of sales staff, the physical number of sales calls that can be made in a day or week, the time taken to process sales orders, the time taken to deliver the goods, inventory levels, supply lead times, ramping-up times, un-planned delays

Budgets are normally set at monthly cycles or intervals, but they can also be set to cover shorter or longer periods. Sales are usually seasonal or they have cyclical patterns and these have to be factored into account. Above all, sales budgets need to be realistic and should recognize that the business and projects can take several months to get going and there are always unplanned problems.

A sale is not a sale until the money is in the bank

Analyzing Sales

Keeping detailed customer and sales records will allow you to analyze these records over a period of time. Keeping them on file will allow you to analyze the following points:

- Which customers buy which products?

- What products sell the most?
- Which products sell the least?
- How does a sales mix change over time?
- How selling prices change over time?
- What trends and cycles develop?
- When customers started or stopped buying certain products?
- What are individual customer cycles?

This information will give you the knowledge you need to revise your marketing strategy and to concentrate on producing better value products.

If your accounting system is well designed, a lot of this information is derived from the analytics that surround Customer Invoices, so attention to Invoice Templates is crucial.

Don't believe sales people: they exaggerate

The 80/20 principle

The common rule of thumb or 'Pareto' principle is found in many instances and this may show that;

- 80% of sales are derived from about 20% of the product range.
- 80% of sales are derived from about 20% of the customer base.

This will conclude that your business is built around 20 % of your total customers and sales are concentrated on about 20 % of your product range. You should be aware of this principle and aim to balance the ratios better, so that they are not skewed. Ideally, a broader customer mix is less risky and this automatically assists with a wider sales spread over more products, so product concentration is diluted.

Sometimes, smaller customers have strategic value if they assist weakening the 80/20 Principle, as they are reducing risk.

Other sales and marketing issues

Other marketing-related issues that should be addressed include:

- Signage
- Marketing material, such as product brochures, displays, product samples, company profiles
- Trading hours
- Advertising mediums and channels
- Web site and on-line channels
- Sales agents
- Product packaging
- Merchandising
- Product launches
- Public relations
- New products
- Product complaints

Case study : location, location and location

A Café had been trading for ten years from premises situated on a busy road in a mixed residential and commercial area. The location was excellent and passing trade was good. However, one of the partners in the Cafe had had a long-standing personality clash with the landlord. After a ten-year tenure, the lease was due for renewal and renegotiation and for a variety of reasons the new terms proposed by the landlord were seen as un-acceptable. Being a little stubborn, the café owners decided to move to a new site literally 100 steps down the road.

The Café owners believed that their loyal customers would walk or drive the extra 100 steps and they were probably correct in their logic. However, within six months the café had closed down. The reason - a brand new Café had taken occupation of the old premises and this new competition meant that one of the Cafés was probably going to fail.

Chapter 7

Margins and Breakeven Analysis

Business involves money management and a successful business owner needs to understand the financial 'basics' in business. There are three critically important business calculations in business and these are:

- Gross profit
- Overheads
- Break-even point

Numbers speak many languages: learn these languages

Gross profit margin

This is the profit left after deducting the cost price from the selling price.

Example 1:

> Selling price is $20
> Cost price is $12
> Gross profit is $8 ($20 less $12)

Example 2:

> Selling price is $75

Cost price is $52.50
Gross profit is $22.50 ($75 less $52.50)

Gross profit is used to pay for overheads. Sales do not pay for overheads. Sales have a role to play, but gross profit is more important. Generally, the more gross profit a business has, the easier it is to pay overheads and make a net profit. A successful business owner will always aim to improve gross profit.

Gross profit is a function of sales and cost of product. You improve gross profit by improving the quality or quantity of the selling price or decreasing the quantity and improving the quality of your cost price, or a combination of all of these.

It is better to sell a product for $ 5 and have $ 3 margin than selling a $ 10 product and having a $ 3 margin.

Gross profit percentage

Gross profit percentage is gross profit divided by selling price, shown as a percentage.

Refer to example 1:

Gross profit is $8 ($20 less $12)
Gross profit percentage is 40% ($8 divided by $20, shown as a percentage)

Refer to example 2:

Gross profit is $22.50 ($75 less $52.50)
Gross profit percentage is 30%
($22.50 divided by $75, shown as a percentage)

Gross profit percentage is also a function of sales and cost of product. You improve gross profit percentage by increasing your selling price or decreasing your cost price, or both.

Weighted (average) gross profit

Businesses rarely sell just one product; their sales are a mix of various products, each which with its own selling price and cost price. Products often have their own unique discount structures and these affect the gross profit calculations too.

A weighted gross profit is the average gross profits which take into account the various products sold and their different selling prices, cost prices and gross profits. Calculating weighted gross profit can appear complicated, but the basic principle is to calculate the average.

For example, a business sells four products – A, B, C and D. The business knows what each product sells for (price) and what each product costs and it can accurately estimate how much of each product makes up the total sales for the business (sales mix).

This information can be summarized as follows:

Product	A	B	C	D
Selling price per item	$20.00	$75.00	$25.00	$30.00
Cost price per item	$12.00	$52.50	$20.00	$20.00
Percentage of total sales	50%	25%	15%	10%

To calculate the weighted gross profit, first calculate the gross profit per product:

Product	A	B	C	D
Selling price per item	$20.00	$75.00	$25.00	$30.00
Cost price per item	$12.00	$52.50	$20.00	$20.00
Gross profit per item	$8.00	$22.50	$5.00	$10.00

Then take the contribution of each product's share of gross profit. Add it up. This is done by taking the gross profit of each product and multiplying it by the sales percentage each product has.

Product	A	B	C	D
Gross profit per item	$8.00	$22.50	$5.00	$10.00
Percentage of total sales	50%	25%	15%	10%
Share of gross profit	$4.00	$5.63	$0.75	$1.00

The weighted gross profit for these four products is $4.00, plus $5.63, plus $0.75, plus $1.00. A total of $11.38.

Weighted (average) selling price

A weighted selling price is the average selling price; the gross profit calculation takes these different selling prices into account. For example, a business sells four products – A, B, C, and D. The business knows what each product sells for, and it can accurately estimate how much of each product makes up the total sales for the business. This information is summarized as follows:

Product	A	B	C	D
Selling price per item	$20.00	$75.00	$25.00	$30.00
Percentage of total sales	50%	25%	15%	10%

Then take the contribution of each product's share of sales and add them up. This is done by taking the selling price of each product and multiplying it by its sales percentage.

Product	A	B	C	D
Selling price per item	$20.00	$75.00	$25.00	$30.00
Percentage of total sales	50%	25%	15%	10%
Contribution of each item	$10.00	$18.75	$3.75	$3.00

The weighted selling price for these four products is $10.00, plus $18.75, plus $3.75, plus $3.00, which equals $35.50.

Weighted gross profit percentage

After calculating the weighted gross profit and the weighted selling price, the weighted gross profit percentage is simply the weighted gross profit divided by the weighted selling price. For example, if the weighted gross profit of products A, B, C and D is $11.38, and the weighted selling price of the same products is $35.50, then the weighted gross profit percentage is 32% ($11.38 divided by $35.50, shown as a percentage)

Mark-up percentage

Having determined a mark-up, it is easy to calculate its percentage. Mark-up percentage is the value of the mark-up itself divided by the original cost of the product. Using the example above, the mark-up percentage would be 67% ($8.00 divided by $12.00, then shown as a percentage).

Mark-up percentages are often used to make pricing simpler. Once a mark-up and its percentage have been determined, you can apply it to pricing similar products. This speeds up the whole pricing process. For example, if you are the owner of a hardware store you will probably only calculate the mark-up on a particular type of nail and its percentage once. After that, you could apply the same – or a similar – mark-up percentage to all other nails you want to sell. It is unlikely you will take each anal and work out each individual mark-up.

The differences in gross profit for products and services

Businesses that buy inventory for resale can quite easily calculate the unit cost for each item. Alternatively, businesses that sell a service don't usually buy 'inventory' as such. They sell unites of time that are sold at market-related or similar rates. For example, professional people such as accountants and attorneys sell a service normally based on an hourly rate. They don't buy inventory; they sell time.

The gross profit of a service-related business is normally 100%. Sales don't have a direct inventory or product cost. The only costs that such a business has are considered overheads. For example, if your selling price is $250 for an hour's service or consultation, and your cost price is zero, then your gross profit is $250, or 100% gross profit percentage.

Why is gross profit so important?

Understanding, determining, analyzing and continually reassessing your gross profit / margins and the linked components are critical in business, for the following reasons:

- Many new business owners believe that sales are the most important thing for their business. This is not entirely true: gross profit is more important. Gross profit / margin is used to pay for overheads. Sales have a role to play, but gross profit is more important.

- Generally, the more gross profit a business makes, the easier it is to pay overheads, and consequently, good net profits are easier to achieve.

- Gross profit is a function of sales and the cost of product sold. You improve gross profit by improving the quality or quantity of your product sales, or by decreasing the quantity of your product costs or increasing the quality of your product costs; or through a combination of one or more of these.

- Small changes in gross profit usually have a large effect on a business's profitability. Any increase in margin usually directly trickles through to Net Profits.

- Comparing gross profit percentages with other, similar businesses can be a useful exercise. You can benchmark your own business, and hopefully find areas where improvements can be made to increase gross profits.

- Every business sector or industry generally has research information and these 'industry averages' often include typical or expected gross profits and gross profit percentages. Large suppliers to the particular business sector or industry usually know this information too.

- Gross profit analysis helps identify products and activities that may require further attention.

One should look at your gross profits on a regular basis, and consider the amount and cost of work that goes into supporting and selling that product. Quite often a business owner will find that the products selling the highest volume are those that create the most work and offer the lowest gross profit. In some cases you may even establish that certain products are being sold at a loss if you factor in all the associated activities and costs that accompany supporting that product.

Overheads

Overheads are the typically recurring, reasonably static expenses that your business will incur every day. They exclude costs for inventory purchases relating to the products that you sell and these costs are taken into account when calculating gross profit.

Typical overheads could include:

- *Accounting.* For services such as registering the business, preparing financial statements, preparing or assisting with statutory returns, preparing tax submissions and possibly contracted bookkeeping activities.
- *Advertising and promotions.* The cost of business and product launches, designing and printing product brochures, product samples to prospective customers, advertising etc.
- *Bad debts.* Monies not collected from customers and which then have to be 'written off'. During the course of a year every business will have some bad debt.
- *Bank charges.* Costs for having and using bank accounts.
- *Communication.* Fixed line and cellular phone costs, fax services etc.

- *Credit card commissions.* Costs paid for processing card related payments made by customers.
- *Delivery and freight.* Costs incurred in delivering products to customers.
- *Depreciation.* This recognizes that business assets are depleted and deteriorate while in use by a business. For tax purposes, certain ratios are used to write off certain assets over a period of time. For example, a vehicle is usually depreciated over a period of five years. This lost value is a form of cost to the business and must be taken into account. While no physical cash is paid out, depreciation on assets is considered an expense to the business.
- *Entertainment.* Those expenses, normally food and beverages purchased to entertain people that are important to the business, such as customers and suppliers.
- *Insurance.* Premiums to protect the business and its broad trading activities including equipment, vehicles, inventory, loss of profits against risks such as fire, burglary and loss. Could also include insurances for key staff, Professional Indemnity, Third Party Claims, Products etc
- *Internet.* Costs for setting up and maintaining a web site, having facilities for e-mail.
- *Interest.* The interest only cost of debt. Can include third party debts and owner loans.
- *Licenses.* Business licenses, Professional licenses etc.
- *Legal fees.* Costs incurred when obtaining legal advice or using legal services. Could include legal costs incurred over a business dispute, recovering bad debts and so on.
- *Maintenance.* Expenses for equipment and business assets including repairs, materials and contractors.
- *Membership costs.* Industry and professional associations.
- *Motor vehicle costs.* Gas and oil and vehicle maintenance.
- *Payroll.* Costs for each person employed by the business. Salaries include not only the amount of cash actually paid

to the staff member/s but also the taxes, insurances, benefits and additional amounts paid to third parties on behalf of the staff member/s. You may wish to consult your Accountant in itemizing Payroll costs as these typically require detailed reporting when submitting Tax returns.

- *Printing and stationery.* Letterheads, business cards and all printed stationery.
- *Rent / Lease.* For leasing your business's premises.
- *Rent / Lease.* For any leased equipment, signage or related assets used by the business.
- *Security.* Costs for security services such as alarm monitoring, armed response, armed guards.
- *Travel.* Air travel, accommodation, car hire whilst traveling on business.
- *Utilities.* Costs associated with the business's premises and the equipment used such as electricity, gas, water, sewer and waste removal.
- *Loan repayments.* Typically loan repayments / instalments do-not get expensed through the Profit and Loan Account. Only the interest portion of the repayment is expensed and the balance is accounted for via the Balance Sheet. At the end of each financial year your accountant will break-down and allocate the repayments / installments between interest and capital. However, for breakeven purposes it is prudent to recognize loan repayments in Breakeven Analysis.

Avoid costs and strive for quality. That's how you make profits

Budgets

You must constantly analyze your overheads; this will allow you to control them more effectively. Areas of excessive expenditure will be identified early, and give you time to take corrective action.

Budgeting is an effective tool in identifying and quantifying overheads and then comparing actual spend to budgeted spend. The differences / variances are then investigated with a view to improvement. Sometimes line items in Budgets require adjustment as they cannot feasibly be reduced and sometimes line items in Budgets have been over-budgeted, so they need to be revised downwards.

Timing your expenditures

Business costs are not always regular. Some expenses occur annually; some are weekly or even daily. When preparing overhead budgets you should consider and identify all costs that will occur over a given period, usually a year. Once annual overheads are determined they can be averaged to a monthly amount. For example, Payroll costs might be $10,000 a month but there is a Bonus due in December of $ 10,000. The correct monthly Payroll cost is therefore $10,833 ($10,000 multiplied by 12, plus the Bonus totals 130,000. This divided by 12 months in 10,833)

If you can't count, don't manage money

Break-even point

Break-even point is the amount of sales revenue or similar measurement that a business or project needs to achieve in order to meet and pay for all its overheads or meet certain obligations. It is the point where a business 'breaks even' financially and it makes neither profit nor a loss.

Knowing your break-even point is a clear sign that you understand the financial aspects of your business or project and that the business is well managed. Keep information about your break-even point confidential.

Calculating the break-even point

Break-even point is calculated as the total overhead costs of the business divided by the gross profit percentage.

Example 1:

Overheads total $40,000 per month
Gross profit percentage is 32%
Break-even point is $125,000 per month ($40,000 divided by 32%)

Example 2:

Overheads total $15,000 per month
Gross profit percentage is 45%
Break-even point is $33,333 per month ($15,000 divided by 45%)

Example 3:

Overheads total $200,000 per month
Gross profit percentage is 67%
Break-even point is $298,507 per month ($200,000 divided by 67%)

Example 4:

Overheads total $75,000 per month

Gross profit percentage is 100% (typical of a service business selling 'time')

Break-even point is $75,000 a month ($75,000 divided by 100%)

Sensitivity and elasticity

The components of break-even include overheads and gross profit percentage. Any changes to either of these components will change the break-even point.

The lower the gross profit percentage the more elastic the break-even point becomes to any overhead or gross profit changes.

Example 1:

Overheads are $40,000 per month

Gross profit percentage is 32%

Break-even is $125,000 per month ($40,000 divided by 32%)

Now, if gross profit drops to 25%, break-even increases to $160,000 per month

($40,000 divided by 25%)

Example 2:

Overheads are $40,000 per month

Gross profit percentage is 32%

Break-even is $125,000 per month ($40,000 divided by 32%)

Now, if overheads increase to $45,000 per month, break-even increases to
$140,625 per month ($45,000 divided by 32%)

Example 3:

Sales person is paid $10,000 per month
Gross profit percentage is 32%
Break-even is $31,250 per month ($10,000 divided by 32%)

Now, if gross profit drops to 25%, break-even increases to $40,000 per month
($10,000 divided by 25%)

Example 4:

Sales person is paid $10,000 per month
Gross profit percentage is 32%
Break-even is $31,250 per month ($10,000 divided by 32%)

Now, if sales person now gets paid $12,000 per month, break-even increases to $37,500 pm ($12,000 divided by 32%)

The higher the gross profit percentage the less elastic the break-even point becomes to any overhead or gross profit percentage changes.

Example 1:

Overheads are $40,000
Gross profit percentage is 72%
Break-even is $55,565 per month ($40,000 divided by 72%)

Now, if gross profit drops to 65%, break-even increases to $61,538 per month
($40,000 divided by 65%)

Example 2:

Overheads are $40,000
Gross profit percentage is 72%
Break-even is $55,565 per month ($40,000 divided by 72%)

Now, if overheads increase to $45,000, break-even increases to $62,500 per
Month ($45,000 divided by 72%)

Example 3:

Sales person is paid $10,000 per month
Gross profit percentage is 72%
Break-even is $13,889 per month ($10,000 divided by 72%)

Now, if gross profit drops to 65%, break-even increases to $15,385 per month
($10,000 divided by 65%)

Example 4:

Sales person is paid $10,000 per month
Gross profit percentage is 72%
Break-even is $13,889 per month ($10,000 divided by 72%)

Now, if sales person now gets paid $12,000 per month, break-even increases to
$16,667 per month ($12,000 divided by 72%)

Case study : $ 5 margin

A small health service partnership was struggling to stay profitable and the two Partners were struggling to earn even small salaries, so they decided to sell. A potential Buyer was interested in purchasing and sought the advice of a consultant. The Buyer wished to purchase the business and still retain the services of the two Sellers as they were medically qualified to continue offering the services that the business sold. The Buyer was not medically qualified and therefore could-not generate direct income for the business, so believed he would concentrate on Business Development activities and find new customers for his staff to service.

The consultant looked at everything and told the Buyer that the business would not succeed, based on the model the Buyer presented. The Buyer disagreed and argued with the consultant and fired him. The Buyer purchased the business, assumed a loan liability to fund part of the purchase transaction and the Sellers happily 'cashed-out' and remained employed earning good hourly rates. The business lasted less than 6 months.

The essence for failure was that the Buyer did-not understand or believe a basic Breakeven Analysis. He had purchased a business that was already struggling and he added significant additional overhead to it by way of his salary and various other new overheads. These new overhead costs increased the required Breakeven Point by some 50 % and this proved impossible. This business model could-not survive on a $ 5 margin.

Using break-even to calculate profits or losses

By knowing the breakeven point, you can calculate your own profit or loss position.

Example 1:

> Overheads are $40,000 per month
> Gross profit percentage is 32%
> Break-even is $125,000 per month ($40,000 divided by 32%)
> If sales are $150,000 per month,
> Profits are $8,000 per month

Calculation: sales of $150,000 multiplied by gross profit percentage of 32% equals $48,000, less overheads of $40,000 equals $8,000.

Example 2:

> Overheads are $40,000 per month
> Gross profit percentage is 32%
>   Break-even is $125,000 per month ($40,000 divided by 32%)
> If sales are $80,000 per month,
> Losses are $14,400 per month

Calculation: sales of $80,000 multiplied by gross profit percentage of 32% equals $48,000, less overheads of $40,000 equals a loss of $14,400.

Example 3:

> Overheads are $15,000 per month

Gross profit percentage is 45%
Break-even is $33,333 per month ($15,000 divided by 45%)
If sales are $40,000 per month,
Profits are $3,000 per month

Calculation: sales of $40,000 multiplied by gross profit percentage of 45% equals $18,000, less overheads of $15,000 equals $3,000.

Example 4:

Overheads are $15,000 per month
Gross profit percentage is 45%
Break-even is $33,333 per month ($15,000 divided by 45%)
If sales are $25,000 per month,
Losses are $3,750 per month

Calculation: sales of $35,000 multiplied by gross profit percentage of 45% equals $11,250, less overheads of $15,000 equals a loss of $3,750.

Why is it so important to know your break-even point?

- It allows you to calculate your profit or loss position at any time. This should be done daily, weekly, fortnightly, and monthly. Through knowing sales, overheads and gross profit margins, one can easily snap-shot and estimate profitability positions.
- It lets you analyze and simplify your sales into daily and weekly targets. For example, if your break-even point is

$125,000 per month, then this can be broken down into a daily target of $5, 682 (22 working days a month) and a weekly target of $28,868 ($125,000 divided by 4.33 weeks a month).

- With this information you can also simplify determine work outputs in manufacturing into daily and weekly targets. The targets will relate to sales and can be broken down into targets per shift and targets per work station.
- It helps you size your business. Knowing a break-even point means you can visualize the level of activity required to achieve that point. Business owners often underestimate the resources required to make a successful business or project.
- It gives you an opportunity to size your competitors. By estimating the overheads of your individual competitors allows you to estimate what their break-even point might be (one assumes you all have similar gross profit margins and if not, make an adjustment). This also helps you in sizing market size, competitor market share etc.
- It allows you to analyze and simplify the cost of certain departments, staff and activities. For example, if a sales person costs the business $10,000 per month, then you need to know what amount of sales that person should be generating to cover his or her own expenses. The value and contribution of certain staff, departments and functions can also bench-marked and questioned.

Taxes and basic business calculations

It's easy to get confused by consumption based taxes and their effect on your business calculations. Generally speaking, taxes paid on purchases and any overhead costs should be included into your calculations and taxes raised on sales should be excluded. You may need advice from your accountant.

Case study : What a deal

The Head Office of a large Group believed that one of their regional branches was running unprofitably, so a decision was made to sell the regional branch to the local management team as a Management Buy-out (MBO) opportunity.

The local managers knew that their Branch WAS profitable. They suspected that the Head Office accounting team were incorrectly allocating costs to their Branch and expenses that didn't belong to them. There was too much Corporate 'paper pushing' going-on.

The local management team did eventually buy the branch at a very low price. The branch went on to prove its profitability – much to the annoyance of the Head Office, which was now left with bigger losses within the Group because they had mistakenly sold one a profitable branch. A simple Break-even analysis is all that it took to determine the correct position of this Branch.

Chapter 8

Cash Flow

What is cash flow?

Cash flow is the <u>source</u>, <u>application</u> and <u>timing</u> of cash. Source: where is the cash coming from? Application: where will it go? Timing: when will it come and go?

The importance of cash

Cash is probably the most critical asset for a business. It pays for goods and services required by the business. Without cash a business cannot trade and a project cannot exist for long. Managing cash flow is critically important.

Cash flow problems are probably the single biggest cause of business failure. Businesses and projects can be profitable on paper but cash flow shortage problems can trigger a sequence of events that lead to business and project failure.

Cash is king; Credit makes a slave

The timing of cash

Most things in life run in cycles and so does cash flow. Cash flow is made up of many sources of cash coming into a business and many applications of cash going out of the business. However, there are certain times within these cycles when the cash flow cycle is at its peak or lowest point.

There are times for big inflows of cash and there are times for big outflows. Managing these inflows and outflows is what cash flow management is all about. Try to balance the inflow and the outflow so that your cash flows 'balance'. You need to identify and quantify the cash flow cycles that affect your business and plan how to react to them.

Usually in businesses, cash flow cycles are weekly and monthly. Larger recurring payments like payroll, payments to suppliers and loan repayments are normally paid at the end of a month and sometimes, mid-month. Similarly, amounts owing to the business are usually collected at the end of the month, or in the first week of the new month.

Normal sources and applications of cash

Sources of cash	Application of cash
Cash received from cash sales	Cash used to pay for overheads
Cash received from debtors / accounts receivables	Cash used to pay suppliers / accounts payables

If the two sources of cash are not enough to fund the two applications, then it is clear that the business has a cash shortage problem that needs to be investigated. Usually the problem will be that the business is not making enough profit. Any shortage of cash then requires an additional source of cash, typically loan and debt funding.

Get – and stay – cash positive

You should aim to ensure that the amount of cash coming into your business exceeds the amount leaving the business. You could simply slow the cash outflows by not paying bills for a short while, leaving you with 'spare' cash. However, this can only be a short-term solution as trading will become difficult as suppliers will discontinue supply services and the business will suffer supply shortages.

Making profits over a long period of time is the single most important cash source. Other sources of cash shortage funding ultimately need to be repaid in one way or another. In the long term, the only way a business can stay cash positive is through making continual profits.

What is the difference between having cash and making a profit?

Profits are a financial calculation. Cash is the physical money available to the business, a physical reality. A business can be making profits but have no cash and similarly, a business can have cash but isn't making a profit.

Profits can be calculated by the owner of the business or his accountant, but cash is determined by the money physically within the control (or likely control) of the business.

Example 1:

> A business sells ten products
> Seven are sold on credit to customers
> Three are sold for cash

Selling price per product is $500

All ten products were purchased from suppliers
Eight were paid for in cash to suppliers
Two bought on account with suppliers
Cost per product is $300
Overheads are $ 678

Profit made

Sales	$5,000 (ten sales at $500 each)
Cost of sale	$3,000 (ten products sold costing $300 each)
Gross profit	$2,000 (sales less cost of goods)
Overheads	$678 (wages, telephone, advertising, delivery)
Profit	$1,322 (gross profit less overheads)

The cash cycle

Cash source	$1,500 (three cash sales at $500 each)
Cash application	$3,078 (eight cash purchases at $300 each $ 2,400, plus overheads $ 678)
Cash available	Shortfall (deficit) of $1,578 ($1,500 less $3,078)

Example 2:

A business sells ten products
Seven are sold on credit to customers
Three are sold for cash
Selling price per product is $500
The business already had the products as inventory – they were paid for

Cost per product is $300

Profit made

Sales	$5,000 (ten sales at $500 each)
Cost of sale	$3,000 (ten products sold costing $300 each)
Gross profit	$2,000 (sales less cost of goods)
Overheads	$678 (wages, telephone, advertising, delivery)
Profit	$1,322 (gross profit less overheads)

The cash cycle

Cash source	$1,500 (three cash sales at $500 each)
Cash application	$678 (only overheads, as products already paid for)
Cash available	Surplus of $822 ($1,500 less $678)

I am making a profit, so where is the cash?

Business owners rarely see their surplus cash amounts and bank accounts physically growing. The eventual fruits of profit do not usually accumulate into hard cash. Profits are usually used by the business to fund expansions, growth and to explore opportunities and never really get a chance to accumulate. Cash is also used to pay income tax, to fund previous losses, prepare for future negative cash flow cycles, to expand the business, purchase more assets, or invest into receivables and inventory. An accountant will show you exactly where your profits go using a Cash Flow Statement or Source and Application of Funds Statement.

The biggest cash receipt you will normally experience is when you sell part or all of your business. This is when the buyer will pay a significant amount of cash to the selling business owner/s. It is one time a business owner really gets to 'feel' the cash rewards from the business.

Preparing a cash flow forecast

A cash flow forecast is a management tool which shows owners, executives or managers what cash flow cycles will look like into the future, should certain assumptions be accurate. A cash flow forecast simply identifies the future amounts and the timing of cash sources and cash applications.

The details making up cash flow are usually what make cash flow look complicated and confusing. Ideally, a cash flow forecast should be done on a computer spreadsheet.

Example of Cash Flow Forecast

Note – 1	Timing	Month 1	Month 2	Month 3	Month ...
2	Cash at start	$1,400	$400	$4,400	
3	CASH INFLOWS				
4	Cash sales	$ 5,000	$8,000	$5,000	
5	Receivables / Collections	$10,000	$15,000	$6,000	
6	Owner funds invested		$ 2,000		
7	TOTAL INFLOW	$15,000	$25,000	$11,000	

8	**CASH OUTFLOWS**				
9	Overheads	$6,000	$7,000	$6,200	
10	Inventory Purchases	$5,000	$6,000	$4,000	
11	Other	$5,000	$8,000	$4,000	
12	**TOTAL OUTFLOW**	$16,000	$21,000	$14,200	
13	**CASH MOVEMEN T**	-$1,000	+$4,000	-$3,200	
14	**Cash at end**	$400	$4,400	$1,200	

The biggest influencers to the forecast are factors totaling Notes 7 and 12 and one can see how the cash flow cycle has swung up and down each month. By forecasting ahead, a good business owner, executive or manager will learn when to manage the cycle to avoid the effects of low cash balances which are risky. This is achieved in managing cash inflows by collecting cash from clients timely and by slowing down and juggling outflows as best as possible.

If outflows are delayed a little, they can be caught-up in subsequent cycles. Sometimes when there are cash shortages, suppliers are leveraged and they are paid late and sometimes even short-paid. Supplier 'credit' elasticity are a common source of funding.

Explanation of notes in cash flow forecast.

Note	Description	Explanation
1	Timing	Timing of cash sources in and cash application out. Could be daily, weekly, monthly, etc.
2	Cash at start of month	Actual cash balances in bank or on hand, which the business has at the start of each timing cycle. This is also the same amount carried Forward from the previous timing period.
3,4,5 ,6	Cash Inflows	Main cash sources from sales and payments from clients, as well as other sources such as cash from business owners.
7	Total Inflow	Total of all cash sources coming into the business within the timing period under consideration (each month) (Add sum of notes 4, 5, 6, to arrive at sum of note 7).
8,9,1 0,11	Cash Outflows	Main cash applications, such as paying overheads, suppliers for inventory, repaying loans, buying equipment, etc. Other could include large repayments towards Loans, Tax Bills and Asset Purchases.
12	Total cash outflow	Total of all cash applications going out of the business within the timing period under consideration (each month). (add sum of notes 9, 10, 11 to arrive at sum of note 12).

| 13 | Cash movement | The surplus or shortfall of cash within the timing period under consideration. It is important to establish if surplus cash was made (cash sources were bigger than cash applications), or if a cash shortfall was incurred (cash sources were smaller than cash applications). (Subtract note 12 from note 7 to arrive at sum of note 13) |
| 14 | Cash at end | Total cash in hand at the end of the period (month), after adding the cash surplus or shortfall made during that period. (Add sum of note 2 to sum of note 13 to achieve this total). |

A cash flow forecast can also be used to plan personal finances. The principles of cash on hand, cash sources, cash applications, cash surpluses/shortfalls and timing periods all apply. The differences are merely in the types of cash sources (salaries, wages, borrowings, etc.) and the types of cash applications (buying food, transport, rent, loan repayments, etc.).

Financing and cash flows

Typically, large acquisitions and asset purchases are not made using cash flow resources. Medium and long-term debt / loan are used to purchase capital items like vehicles, manufacturing equipment etc.

These items are then repaid over time. Typically movables (vehicles, equipment, fittings, furniture, computer, equipment etc) are financed with debt that is repayable between 3 and 5 years. The purchase of real estate is typically financed with debt that is repayable between 10 and 20 years.

The shorter the repayment period, the larger the repayment instalment will be, as the capital portion of the instalment is higher than the interest cost portion. The difference between repaying a 20 or 30 year real estate debt (mortgage) is not that significant and a shorter term is recommended as this will save interest costs.

Do-not be tempted to finance movable asset purchases using cash flow resources. Rather get financing and balance your Balance Sheet.

Rapid growth, expansions, new projects, new product lines, inventory purchases, a change in credit policies to customers and by suppliers etc can also trigger a need for more cash resources and short term working capital financing is recommended for this.

Working capital financing can be traditional bank credit lines, owner loans / equity and lesser known sources such as factoring and invoice discounting.

If term finance is being used to fund cash flow shortages that are resulting from low / no profits, this is a big risk.

Chapter 9

Marketing

Holistically, marketing is probably the most important activity for any business.

Define your market

Defining your market forces the business to better understand who customers will / might be. Once you know this, you can then;

- Establish what market-share you need to achieve your break-even point. This will always be an estimate but the more market share you need to survive, the riskier this position is.
- Identify your competition, research them and better understand them. Researching competitors, their business practices, where they advertise, how they differentiate etc is critical.
- Once you know who is going to possibly buy your products and services, you can also start profiling these customers and breaking them into sub-groups as sometimes the sub-groups have subtle differences and they require a different marketing mix and approach.
- Identify what the differentiators are / or those required by the business that can be leveraged for success.
- Identify strengths, weaknesses, opportunities and threats in your market/s. Markets change all the time and it is critical that you stay abreast and adjust to these changes.

- Identify product life cycles. Every product has a life cycle starting with development, growth, maturity and decline. Between maturity and decline, the product needs attention and re-development and reinventions so that the maturity phase is extended and even better, a new growth phase is created. Good examples are automobiles, models are refreshed and re-designed every couple of years to retain market share and to extend the maturity phase.

Businesses often have a primary market, from where most of their business will come from but there are always secondary markets which sometimes offer good potential with just small changes in the marketing mix.

The marketing mix and the Four P's

The basics of marketing involve the traditional Four P's;

- Product
- Price
- Promotion
- Place

Product refers to what the business is offering for sale to customers who are the target market. Products / services have to be really competitive and good, if not excellent and they should be positively differentiated from those of the competition. Product needs to satisfy as many customer needs and wants as possible as competition is fierce and customers have choices. Other factors associated to Products / services are life cycle, product range, packaging, quality, features, warranties, after sales, recycling, recalls.

Price refers to the monetary value (price) the customers are being asked to pay for the product / service they need and or want. What the customer wants to pay is not always what they need to pay. If the price gap between what the customer wants to pay and what they need to pay is too big, a sale is unlikely to take place. Price has a strong relationship with cost and the difference between price and cost is 'margin'. Margin is a critical determinant in break-even analysis. The less margin, the more volume you have to sell. Price, cost, margin and sales volume all have a connected elastic relationship and you need to know the elasticity between these variables. Other factors associated to Price are sales terms (cash / credit), discount structures, ease of payment (cards, cash, checks etc), the frequency of price changes.

Promotion refers to communicating the actual / real and / or perceived benefits and value of product to customers. This also requires persuading potential new customers to become new customers of your business using methods such as advertising, cold calling, referrals, being visible, publicity and promotion. Different products require different Promotion strategies.

Place refers to all the different channels and ways of physically getting product to customers. This includes the location of your business, the shop front, signage, distribution channels (retail, distributors etc), logistics and transportation, internet sales, deliveries and returns.

An excellent product can fail if the marketing mix is not well balanced and a poor product can still succeed if the marketing mix is well balanced.

Sales prices

A huge temptation for businesses is experimenting with selling prices, especially if;

- The business is new. Generally managers will be concerned not to start with prices that are too high as a reputation can quickly build that the business is 'expensive'. It may be prudent to start with lower prices and be to adjust pricing upwards as the business grows and demand gets stronger.
- The business is not doing well. One of the first things businesses do when they start getting into trouble is to lower prices in the hope that this stimulates demand and increases sales. Most times, lowering prices alone doesn't help and several strategies are required if there is to be improvement. Lowering prices means that margins are eroded, so higher volumes need to be sold to replace 'lost' margin. Dangerous.
- Trying to capture market share. Business strategy could be to lower prices in an attempt to gain market share. Typically strategies like this are used if the business is targeting competition, or if the business enjoys a cost or overhead advantage. Growing market share through price manipulations is often a short-term strategy and once market share is secured, prices tend to drift upwards again.
- Competition is increasing and demand and sales are falling. Generally, the more competitors a business has the more prices are under downward pressure. This situation places all competitors under stress and this can trigger a downward spiral for the whole market that affects all competitors. Covert 'collusion' between competitors to manipulate prices to save markets under duress can become an option, but this is risky.

- Demand is strong. If demand becomes too strong, supply issues can lead to prices increase. This is basic economics. Sometimes businesses are selling so well that they raise prices as strategy to dampen demand slightly.
- Cost push drivers force regular adjustments to sell prices so that margins are preserved. Examples are crude oil and metals that have daily market price fluctuations, so downstream products made from these crude source materials may have regular price changes.
- In economies where there is significant inflation, it becomes a habit to adjust prices in order to preserve margins. Businesses incur inflationary cost increases in their overheads and cost of sales variables, so these need to 'passed onto' the customer. Businesses that fail to adjust sell prices to cover inflationary erosion will suffer a decline in margin and profitability.

It is critical that sales prices be well thought-out and strategized before they go to market as 'Margin' determines success or failure. Errors and mistakes with sell prices and margin are extremely costly.

Be different – identify and leverage differentiators

A key factor to succeeding in any business is having real or perceived 'differentiators'. These differentiators are what make you different and more appealing to customers. Differentiators also put barriers between you and your competition. The more differentiators you have, the stronger the business.

Differentiators can include a combination of the following;

- Motivated employees and managers. People are the key assets and catalysts. Bad employees and managers will never make any business successful.
- Exceptional service through-out the customer experience cycle. Listen, treat the customer right, be respectful, be knowlegible and be fast. Service is one of the least 'expensive' differentiators a business can have as it typically relies on employees to provide and deliver.
- Being so customer focused that customers choose your business just because you are so 'nice'.
- Be flexible. Push for a positive outcomes even if it means compromising or bending or breaking some rules.
- Having truly unique and different products. Even if you have similar products to your competitors, do something different with them just to be different.
- Really competitive price points. Consider loss leaders and have keen prices on the really competitive products but try secure margin claw-back on other less competitive products.
- Wide product range and choices. Customers like choices. Offering choices also requires investment in inventory and a lot of inventory means that turnover ratios will soften. Too much inventory brings other problems, so get a balance.
- Location, accessibility, visibility and parking. Be accessible and make it easy for the customer reach-out, find you and get to you.
- Technology advantages. Businesses invested in slick technologies need to leverage this strength and opportunity before it changes. Technologies change fast.
- Specialization and/or expert skills in your industry. Specialization, where possible is a good differentiator and it usually allows the business to charge higher prices.

- Look and act differently. Cleanliness, pleasant environmental conditions, safety, uniforms, strong branding, eloquent speech and written skills all raise the bar between you and your competition.

Understand your market and your competitors really well and then decide what differentiators you can possibly leverage so that you stand-out from the crowd. Think like a customer.

Advertising and branding

Every business needs to advertise and advertising is not always a cheap spend. Trying to determine your return on investment for an advertising budget spend is usually more subjective than quantifiable. However, not advertising at all is going to cost the business way more in the long run. Marketing and advertising are two different things.

Typically businesses spend between 2 % and 10 % of their total overhead costs on advertising. This may fluctuate as strategies change. New businesses sometimes spend more as they are under start-up pressure to secure sales and market share and older established businesses may spend less as they have word of mouth and referrals that have grown over time and their advertising is more brand reinforcement based.

The most effective advertising is word of mouth referrals. This form of advertising is very powerful and it can work for you, or against you. If you are bad, customers will tell more others and way quicker than if you are good.

Analyze your competitors and see where and how they advertise and learn from it, so that you can create your own advertising strategy and budgets leveraging your differentiators and strengths. Advertising is a big industry. Be cautious experimenting with new advertising mediums as you can easily spend and not have much to show for it too.

A lot of marketing experts believe that regular and repetitive advertising is better than larger and less frequent advertising, so rather plan a smaller but regular campaign than bigger ones that are less frequent. Be patient and confident. Decide on what you want to do and stick to it for at least 3 months before judging it. The conversion cycle between advertising and getting new customers can sometimes be long but when it starts working it becomes a steady stream

Try as best as you can to track which advertising delivered your new customers. Ask the new customers why they are transacting with you. Also ask your advertisers for help and tips on how to track new customers to specific advertisements. This all helps determine where spend is best allocated.

Invite complaints. I know this sounds strange but customer complaints are a good source of information if the business wishes to satisfy customer needs and wants in the long term. Do-not take criticism or negative feedback unprofessionally. Rather, encourage it and study what the messages are. Not all customers are right all the time, so sometimes the complaints are unjustified or there is little you can actually do to change things. However, the more you can correct and fix things that are broken, the better. Great businesses invest a lot in obtaining customer feedback and analyzing it so that they can fix what needs to be fixed.

Case Study: Doubling sales within 18 months

I once owned a removals and storage business that had traded for nearly 20 years. The previous owner did very little advertising and branding was weak. The business had tenure and an established customer base but growth was stagnant. I knew that any improvement in sales would trickle in a fat margin to the bottom line as overheads were reasonably inelastic and existing sales covered all my costs.

I did a few key simple differentiators that helped double sales within 18 months and these included;

- *Advertising budget. I spent 10 % of my sales on advertising. I invested into the future and it worked for me. I had to advertise in the Yellow pages as that is where all my competitors advertised (industry standard) and I needed to be right up front where the larger competitors placed themselves. Previously less than 2 % of sales was spent on advertising.*
- *I improved the Website and when-ever we did a removals, we dropped flyers into the post boxes around the site where we had just worked.*
- *Branding. I had removals trucks professional wrapped / sign written along the sides and back and offered 'Fast Free Estimates'. I chose a cartoon like logo (a Dalmatian dog) as part of my 'brand' so that my trucks became easily identifiable. Customers didn't always remember my business name but they always remembered my cartoon character Dalmatian or doggy. I leveraged a mental 'tag'.*
- *Being neat and tidy. I also ensured that every employee wore corporate branded clothing and we washed and cleaned these every day at the business. The premises*

and trucks where always clean. We looked sharp and smart and we stood out.

- *Fast Free Estimates. Most of my competitors made it difficult for customers in so many ways when doing an Estimate for a Customer. We didn't. We did it over the phone, added a little extra volume as customers always under-estimated what they needed and we turned these Estimates around within an hour. We made Estimates as easy as possible for the Customer and we padded a little so that we didn't lose any margin.*

- *Offered discounts. We never offered discounts up front. We only offered discounts about 2 days after we gave a customer an estimate and if we hadn't heard from the customer yet. On Day 2 or Day 3 we offered up to 20 % discount on condition the customer accepted our revised scheduling appointment. The industry trick with removals is that if you can complete a job in the morning and a second job in the afternoon, the second job is pretty much 90 % margin as the biggest cost is your labor and this is priced / costed into the first job. Performing a discounting second job was still way profitable than no second job at all.*

- *Added new markets. The business previously did very little corporate / commercial work, so we started targeting these types of customers offering removals and truck and driver hire. The work was more intensive and required more skills but it paid better and it was a 'new' market for us and we didn't really need to adjust our marketing mix much to get into this market. We eventually secured a large annual contract for a large government agency too.*

Mainly due to these changes, sales doubled within 18 months and the business underwent a rapid growth phase. Profits grew and It was good in many ways. How many small marketing changes could be made to your business that could potentially boost your profits?

Chapter 10

Manufacturing

In most businesses, manufacturing activities and resources account for the highest overhead costs and capital investment. Overheads are largely labor costs and additional expenses such as rentals, maintenance, health and safety, training and consumables. Capital investment is into manufacturing equipment, cranes, forklifts, storage systems, materials handling, environmental control (heat, humidity, noise etc), recycling and related manufacturing infrastructure.

It is important to have a well-managed manufacturing line, as this is usually where the greatest savings and losses can occur in a business. Manufacturing entails producing finished goods by using labor, processes and materials. Each of these resources adds value (and cost) to the final product.

What are my resources?

Manufacturing activities require resources. You must establish what resources are needed in order to produce. These may include:

- Materials
- Processes
- Labor
- Equipment
- Systems
- Intellectual property

Materials

Materials generally include items that are used to make a finished product. These may include raw materials, sub-assemblies, components, consumables, packaging and labeling. You need to investigate and establish the constituent parts of your finished product. Once these individual components have been established, you can identify sources of supply. This is achieved through purchasing activities.

Processes

Goods are produced using certain processes. These may include manual labor, specialist techniques, equipment functions and chemical reactions. Establish what processes are required for the various materials so that they can be processed into finished goods. These steps should be documented into Standard Operating Procedures (SOP's) so that each process can be carefully duplicated without any change to the finished product.

Labor

No manufacturing activity can occur without labor. Labor may be categorized according to skill levels: unskilled, semi-skilled and skilled. Ascertain what skills are required during each of the manufacturing processes and match suitable labor in the right quantity and quality to that process. On-going training is a high need as is skills development across various work stations.

Equipment

Equipment is used to perform certain processes which manual labor cannot perform, or which are performed more effectively, efficiently and consistently than labor. When choosing equipment you should consider:

- *What is your equipment going to be doing?* Equipment generally performs select primary functions and perhaps certain secondary functions. You should only purchase equipment that performs the functions that are required for your product. Often, the secondary functions offered by a piece of equipment may never be used and may actually be a waste of money.

- *How much does it cost?* This includes the direct cost of the equipment from the supplier as well as other indirect costs such as accessories, customized tools, transportation and delivery, rigging, commissioning, calibrating, trial runs and waste.

- *Will there be maintenance costs*? Certain manufacturers may sell equipment at a relatively low price and look to charge high prices for repairs, parts and maintenance items (computer printers are a good example). The frequency of maintenance procedures and the cost of labor and materials need to be established and taken into account. Procedures during maintenance must also be established, as often equipment cannot work while it is being serviced. This stoppage will cost the business in lost manufacturing time.

- *Quality*? Compare similar models from the various manufacturers of the equipment. Certain manufacturers may specialize and have a reputation for building higher-quality machines. Cheaper is normally 'cheap' and ultimately costs more in the long run.

- *New or used?* In most instances used equipment may appear to be cheaper, but indirect costs such as repairs, higher maintenance costs, accessories, tools, decommissioning, transportation and delivery will increase costs, closing the gap on new equipment.

- *Specialization* The more specialized a piece of equipment is, the fewer manufacturers will be making it. This could mean that the equipment will have a higher purchase price and that it will be more expensive to maintain and repair.

- *Output capacity?* It is critical to establish and verify equipment capacity. How many, how much and in what time. Be conservative when calculating equipment capacities and rather have equipment with spare capacity than something that will operate too close to its maximum capacity.

- *Longevity?* All equipment has a certain useful life span. For tax purposes, equipment usually has accelerated write-off periods compared to real-life deprecation periods. Always establish the expected economic life of the equipment.

- *What is its overall condition?* The condition of the equipment takes into account physical appearance, hours worked, maintenance history, use and abuse. Equipment suppliers are a good source of reference when trying to evaluate the overall condition of a used piece of equipment.

- *Is there a supporting network?* The availability and reputation of the suppliers and agents selling and supporting the equipment need to be ascertained. Suppliers with poor service levels may cost in the long run if manufacturing is at a standstill while you are waiting for service support. The cost of this support needs to determined. The more specialized the skills and the less suppliers of the skill-set means higher costs.

- *Warranties?* Establish what kind of warranties the manufacturer and the supplier can offer and what after-sales support is available. After-sales support could include training, parts and components, access to loan equipment and the use of equipment during trials.

- *Scrapping?* When equipment needs to be scrapped there may be decommissioning costs such as rigging, transportation and scrapping permits.

- *Calibration?* Equipment needs to be accurate. If it's relevant to your manufacturing process, calibration needs to be done on a regular basis in order to ensure that your manufacturing specifications and standards are consistently accurate and achieved. Equipment that is incorrectly calibrated causes wastage and cost.

Systems

The systems used in manufacturing are critical. They should be as efficient and effective as possible. Good systems will save time and money and poor systems add cost. When considering and designing systems you should bear the following points in mind:

- Quantify your targets. Manufacturing targets are linked to sales targets. That is to say, you make what you sell. Analyze your sales budgets as these form the starting point for your manufacturing targets. These goals should also be linked to manufacturing time periods (shifts or days).

   For example:

   (a) Your sales budget are 400 units a month. Assume that 5% are rejected; then a further 20 units must be produced to cover this eventuality.
   (b) There are normally 22 working days in a month, but assume that 15% of this time is lost to equipment downtime, repairs or maintenance. A further 60 units are required to cover this.
   (c) In order to operate at 80% efficiency, therefore, the monthly manufacturing target is actually 480 units, or 21.8 units per day.

- *Establish your workstations.* These are physical areas where resources are grouped together to produce output.

Workstations should perform similar activities. Identify which workstations are required and what resources will be allocated to each station.

- *Determine layouts and work flows.* Layouts refer to the physical location of each workstation in relation to the other. Every workstation will have an input and an output. They should be laid out so that the output of one workstation is close to the input of the next workstation. An efficient layout creates efficient workflow.

- *Determine minimum and maximum outputs.* The total output of each resource within a workstation should be quantified. Make allowances for work stoppages, interruptions, failures and human error. 'Balancing the line' is the Target.

- *Measure labor output.* The output of individual and collective labor out should be measured and analyzed. This will allow you to evaluate efficiency and performance, both individually and collectively.

- *Measure equipment output.* The output of individual and collective equipment should be measured and analyzed. This will allow you to evaluate efficiency and performance, both individually and collectively.

- *Measure rejects and wastage.* Rejects are goods that do not meet set quality standards. Sometimes rejects can be reworked or they offer recoveries. In principle, rejects add cost. Rejects should be measured as part of your general performance evaluation. Wastage is goods that cannot be reworked or recovered and are normally pure cost to a business. Wastage cannot always be avoided, but uses for waste should be identified.

- *Data analysis.* Collect and analyze manufacturing-related data wherever physically and economically possible. This will allow you to measure, analyze, evaluate and take corrective action, thereby improving manufacturing.

- *Balancing.* Workstations do not produce at smooth regular outputs. Processes change, efficiencies change, systems evolve, different work shifts give different outputs and there is human error. All these factors continually influence manufacturing. It is important to learn to manage and control manufacturing efficiency by re-allocating resources from one workstation to another and managing outputs so that lines are balanced.
- *Minimize handling and travelling.* Goods used in manufacturing processes should be handled as little as possible and they should travel as little as possible. Handing and travelling use time and add cost. The design and layout of your workstation need to take this into account.
- *Avoid bottlenecks.* Bottlenecks are caused when the output of a certain workstation is too slow. Bottlenecks should be identified as soon as possible and corrected. Normally these occur due to a sharp drop in efficiency from one or more of the resources used in that workstation. With the start of a new layout there are often bottlenecks because manufacturing is not yet balanced.
- *Determine minimum manufacturing runs.* There is normally a minimum quantity / run that can be produced economically. This minimum quantity takes into account the time and various costs associated with setting up a line, getting inventory, organizing labor and so on. Try to establish the minimum quantity before manufacturing starts. The longer a run lasts, the better as efficiencies are maintained.

Manufacturing terms

Terms are given in manufacturing to describe how goods are made. These three general descriptions are:

Job

Where a product is produced one unit at a time. For example, boats are built one at a time.

Batch

A group of products are produced at one time. For example, a bottle manufacture will make a certain quantity of a particular style / shape of bottle.

Continuous

Where similar products are made all the time without changes. These are for products that are high volume and need long production runs as sales volumes are high.

Lead times

A business produces goods based on its planned expectations of selling them. Consequently, manufacturing targets and plans are normally derived from marketing plans and sales budgets. However, getting products ready for sale takes a certain amount of time. You need to factor in time for the following activities:

- Determining what finished goods are required
- Determining when finished goods are required
- Getting quotations and cost estimates
- Costing the finished goods

- Placing purchase orders with suppliers
- Waiting on suppliers to deliver
- Taking delivery of goods
- Working the goods through various manufacturing processes
- Unplanned stoppages and line disruptions

Time can be further absorbed by factors such as late deliveries by suppliers and delays in manufacturing. It is therefore important for you to accurately determine the various time components associated with manufacturing your products. A timely and consistent supply of finished goods for resale is critical. Not having finished goods to sell obviously costs the business in terms of lost sales and lost opportunities and having too much inventory and money tied up in that inventory also costs.

Health and safety

Manufacturing activities usually account for the majority of work-related injuries and sicknesses. Your business needs to comply with relevant health, occupational and safety standards. Ensure that all manufacturing activities are as safe as possible and as healthy as possible. Injuries and sickness caused by manufacturing activities will cost a business directly and indirectly.

Outsourcing

Outsourcing is growing in popularity and sometimes it is more viable to outsource than self-manufacture. Outsourcing can offer the following benefits;

Customer and sales focus. Businesses that are heavily invested with manufacturing activities easily find that the 'factory' or manufacturing business units start setting the pace, influencing policy and business focus. This is backward. Customer and sales are the focal points and manufacturing follows the market.

Reduction in capital investment. Manufacturing resources are no longer required as these are performed by contracted third parties who invest in manufacturing resources.

Cash boost. By closing down manufacturing, there will be a cash boost as manufacturing resources are sold and liquidated. Overheads will also decrease.

Focus into core activities. The business can now focus on fewer core activities as there are less activities to manage.

Nimbleness. The business downsizes in head-count and activity levels after outsourcing and this can promote nimbleness. Manufacturing is cumbersome, generally quite labor and capital intensive.

Access to expert skills. Outsourcing manufacturers generally offer Subject Matter Expert skills as they have a passion for manufacturing and they do it well, so let them do it.

Chapter 11

Purchasing and Quality

Purchasing

Holistically, managed purchasing is very important considering that the total costs that a business will pay for in a year. Even a 2 % saving equates into substantial money and there is always scope for improvement, new price negotiations, better terms and conditions and better quality for the same price.

Product costs have a direct effect on gross profit margins and required sell prices. Businesses should aim to purchase correctly so that product costs are as economical as possible. Factors to be considered when purchasing include the following:

- *Determining what needs approval before purchasing.* Managing the purchase of small cost items is a no brainer. Too many businesses invest more time and effort in approving a $ 50 spend and this is inefficient. Rather audit a random sampling of small dollar purchases than have a heavy approval system.
- *Concentrating purchasing.* Purchasing should be a specialized management function and not left to low level employees.
- *Obtaining estimates.* Suppliers need to submit written estimates for items required by your business. The requests made to the suppliers should be in writing and they should accurately describe and detail what exactly is required.

- *Analyze supplier quotations and estimates.* Once quotes and estimates are in hand they should be compared to the original requests you made, as well as compared between suppliers. Care should be taken to establish that there are no misunderstandings. Issues which require consideration include price, quality, after-sales service, guarantees, return policies, price validity periods or variables, and conditions of sale.

- *Determine direct and indirect costs.* All costs associated with a purchase should be identified and quantified. Direct costs include the actual cost of the goods or services, and indirect costs include delivery, couriers, insurance, handling fees, and storage fees.

- *Seek credit.* Paying for purchases using supplier credit terms obviously assists with cash flow but is also offers a strategic position to withhold payment should you need to 'renegotiate' with a supplier. Often, paying cash for goods and services moves you to a weaker position when it comes to negotiation. They may be issues with the service or product supplied and by not having yet paid the supplier, this forces him to become attentive and negotiable.

- *Approved suppliers.* An 'Approved Suppliers' list should be available through-out the business. This saves time and money.

- *Placing orders.* Ordered placed for the delivery of goods and services should wherever possible be put in writing and signed by authorized staff. By issuing written orders you will be able to monitor and control purchases more easily.

- *Economic order quantities.* Suppliers generally price their goods with price breaks for varying quantities and it is important to ask suppliers what these price breaks are and leveraging. Be careful not to over-purchase and then have redundant inventory.

- *Tracking orders.* Orders placed with suppliers should be tracked and monitored. Often suppliers with long delivery lead times experience problems and quoted delivery dates get extended and this has consequences for the business. It is important to know as soon as possible if deliveries may be delayed so that corrective action can be taken.

- *Accepting delivery of goods.* Goods delivered by suppliers should first be inspected before being accepted. Once you accept delivery, you forfeit certain legal rights. If the goods are not correct, then don't accept delivery by signing for them. Often an incorrect quantity is delivered, goods may be damaged or the goods are just the wrong goods.

- *Timing of deliveries.* Establish from each supplier what their accounting cycles are. By doing this, you can maximize your credit period by ordering goods but only taking delivery early in the new accounting month. This allows some extended credit eg, if a suppliers accounting cycle is calendar month and he has offered you 30 day terms, get the goods delivered early in the new month and this means you only pay for them at the end of the next month. This credit manipulation helps you cash-flow cycle.

- *Returning goods.* Sometimes goods delivered by a supplier need to be returned. Usually suppliers do not like accepting returns. They charge a handling fee on all goods returned and they also take a long time passing an accounting credit or refund.

- *Defective goods.* It is important to account for all defective goods so that it is known where, when and how these goods were purchased and to ensure the purchase is not repeated. Defective goods cost a business. They incur unnecessary handling costs and interfere with production. Defective goods re-sold to customers create poor relations and incur additional costs.

- *Production plans.* Purchasing activities are largely influenced by the planned consumption needs of manufacturing activities. There must always be good communication between manufacturing and purchasing so that materials and goods required by manufacturing are supplied correctly and timeously. Manufacturing plans and related information are critical for purchasing to be effective; this information should be made available to the purchasing department in good time so that lead times are not compromised.

- *Urgent and crisis orders.* Despite thorough planning, it frequently happens that certain goods and materials are not available when required. Deliveries get delayed, suppliers have stock-outs, staff forget to order, purchasing orders get misplaced. Urgent and crisis orders are disruptive to the business, as other planned work is ignored and additional costs are incurred.

- *Internal issues of goods.* Internal issues involve goods and materials supplied and released from internal stores into manufacturing. Goods and materials issued internally should be counted and recorded as they ultimately influence inventory records and manufacturing records.

Buying right allows you to make and sell right

Inventory control

Inventory control aims to establish why, where and how much inventory the business has. Inventory comes in various forms and can include raw materials, sub-assemblies, semi-completed goods (work in progress),

It is important to control inventory in order to prevent theft or wastage, improve purchasing and costing method and make the maximum use of business funds by not having too much inventory or by having the wrong or redundant inventory.

Aim to control your inventory by keeping records which determine your theoretical inventory-holding position as well as the actual physical inventory holding. These records should be kept current and accurate at all times. Basically, whatever materials and goods have been purchased by your business should either have been sold or be physically sitting in inventory somewhere. There are always discrepancies between actual and theoretical inventory levels and they need to be investigated.

Physical inventory counts often expose variances and discrepancies in inventory. The reasons for this can include.

- *Human error.* So much activity is associated with inventory that human error becomes a real issue.
- *Incorrect counting and classification.* Notwithstanding inaccurate counting or classifying, if the physical item is actually still with the business, then there is no real loss. However, it is important to count and classify as accurately as possible.
- *Theft or shrinkage.* Inventory theft normally involves employees. It is a loss control risk that all business owners need to be aware of.
- *Wastage.* Every business incurs wastage, but it is important to keep it to a minimum. Continually consider new work methods and processes.
- *Calibrations.* Measurement tools and devices become inaccurate with use over time and need to be calibrated on a regular basis. If measurements are incorrect, then costings become incorrect as the physical quantity of inputs into

finished goods has changed and doesn't agree with that originally planned. Incorrect calibrations influenced the quality and cost of products.

Inventory levels

Holding inventory costs money. These costs include the direct cost of the goods or materials and indirect costs such as shrinkage, bank interest, lost opportunity cost, storage space etc. Other costs include obsolete / redundant inventory which is inventory no longer required by the business due to changes in sales or production processes.

The cost of holding too little inventory includes ordering uneconomic quantities, delays in production (because there are no goods) and lost sales. A customer cannot buy a product if it is not available. Alternatively, if suppliers are unreliable and goods and supplies are not readily available you may be forced to carry high inventory levels.

Inventory turnover

Inventory turnover relates to the rate at which inventory is sold. This rate is normally expressed in days or months and takes into account inventory levels and sales levels. For example if 10 units are sold every month and on average there are 15 units in inventory, then the 'inventory turnover' is 15 divided by 10, multiplied by the number of days in the month. The inventory turnover is therefore 45 days.

Generally, the quicker the inventory turnover, the more efficient the business and the less likely that it will be overstocked. But it stands more risk of being out of inventory. Calculate the inventory turnover of various products within the product range in order to keep a grip on your inventory and production levels.

The 80/20 principle

The principle as it relates to inventory is that:

- 80% of sales will be derived from about 20% of the business's inventory.
- 20% of the sales will be derived from about 80% of the business's inventory.

You should be aware of this principle and aim to balance the ratios better by selling products that account for a lower percentage of total sales. Sales should ideally be balanced so that the business has more potential customers and more target markets.

Quality

Quality is the rating or grading given to a product or service after comparing its various characteristics with competitor products or services and industry standards.

Determining quality standards

It is important to establish what quality standards you want your products and services to adhere to. Similar products with quality standards may appeal to different target markets. After analyzing a competitor's products and understanding industry standards for quality, a business will be able to determine the various quality standards that it chooses to uphold.

Consistency

Once a quality standard has been determined, keep that standard consistent. Quality standards should not differ from product to product, or from batch to batch. Customers need assurance that the product purchased last time will be the same purchased the next time. Poor consistency in any business causes customer dissatisfaction. Products must conform within certain tolerances to a consistent standard and products not meeting this standard should be rejected.

Reference samples

Keep samples of products as reference points against which future products can be measured. Perceptions change over time. Reference samples should be kept in a secure place and there should be a sufficient quantity of them for future use as they be dismantled, examined and taken apart. Keep a register for them to track movement in / out.

Testing policies and procedures

It is worth formulating a test policy, where products are examined during the various stages of production. Tests should entail physical inspection and further 'tests'. All materials and products constituting a finished product should be tested. This implies that goods received from suppliers should be tested, as well as goods in the production process and goods returned from customers. Test procedures and methods should be as consistent as possible, as any changes will obviously affect the outcome of test results. Tests could be performed by qualified staff within your business or by suitably qualified external staff.

Certification

Consider third-party certification as a means of enhancing product appeal to target markets. These certifications include markings that the industry and public accept as a high standard or quality level. In certain industries certification is critical as the industry seeks to regulate itself, normally for statutory reasons. Examples include International Standards Organization (ISO) certification. Various industries have generally accepted certification standards and it is important to know them and apply them.

Defects and rejects

Products that do not meet quality standards are defective and become rejects. It is sometimes possible to 'rework' the product so that it may pass subsequent tests and be approved. It is also important to identify reasons why defects occur and every effort should be made to prevent future occurrences. Defects and rejects add cost. Defective goods should be kept in a separate store area and destroyed or removed only after a certain time.

Keeping records and statistics

If you choose to implement quality procedures in your business, then you will need to keep accurate records of inputs, outputs, defects and customer returns. These records need to be analyzed and statistics formulated in order to assist you in measuring performance. For example, you will need to know if your defect rate on a certain product was 2% one month but had risen to 5% a month later. These statistics provide information with which to manage the business better.

Serializing and markings

Products sold by a business should be serialized and marked so that one can identify them as having been legally sold, whom they were sold to and the date and time of manufacture. Information like that is necessary to keep track of product guarantees, returned goods and product recalls. A business may have manufactured a batch of defective products that initially passed quality test but were later found to be defective. It might be necessary to recall these products from customers and replace them.

Good quality makes money. Poor quality loses money

Chapter 12

Administration and Finance

Administration in business normally refers to those back office type activities that are required to keep the business functioning. Administrative functions usually involve the creation, handling, filing and maintenance of documentation and records received and generated by the business. These typically include:

- *Hardcopy mail.* Incoming and outgoing
- *Reception area.* Customers, suppliers, visitors.
- *Switchboard.* Incoming, outgoing and internal telephone calls; message-taking.
- *Faxes.* Incoming and outgoing.
- *Typing resource.* Letters, documents, reports, etc.
- *Filling.* Correspondence, suppliers' invoices and records.
- *Internal mail.* Memos, reports, publications, internal orders.
- *Employee records.* Time sheets, attendance register, leave, sick leave, salary slips.
- *Employee personal records.* Employment contracts, CVs, IDs, drivers' licenses.
- *Meetings.* Taking minutes, circulating agendas and notices.
- *Office supplies.* Stationary, refreshments, canteen supplies, toiletries.

The design and choice of an administrative system in small business are usually quite simple and influenced by the nature of the company and the preferred work methods of the staff member(s) responsible for these duties. The various functions are relatively simple work tasks, but they need to be inspected and checked on a regular basis.

Document confidentiality and security

An important consideration for any administration system is document confidentiality and security. Only authorized persons should have access to relevant documentation and only senior trusted persons should be able to access really sensitive and confidential documentation. While it is difficult to ensure confidentiality and security at all times, a system should be in place to protect hard copy records and soft copy records on computer files. Safe storage and back-up copies of records is vital.

Disposal of records is also important and shredding hardcopy documentation is recommended.

Check your dustbins. It's not all rubbish

Archiving Records

Daily documents and records should be kept for a minimum of five years, while anything involving government authorities should be kept for ten years. Keeping all these historical records requires the development of an archiving and storage system whereby documents can be stored and accessed when needed. In small businesses these records are usually kept in their original form and need not be processed or scanned into computer format (PDF, JPEG, TIF etc).

Ideally archived records they should be kept off the business premises, as this protects them from loss or damage as a result of a fire, water, weather etc. A filing register needs to be maintained in order to track records entering and leaving the archive.

This functions can be professionally outsourced as reasonable cost.

Office and computer equipment

Office equipment includes all physical equipment used by a small business to support its administration and accounting systems. Identify what your equipment needs are; make decisions about what equipment to purchase, rent or lease. Allocate the use of the equipment and the responsibility for it to staff members who are competent enough to manage it so that it functions correctly and is properly maintained. Computer systems usually require special skills not always available within the business and will often entail contracting outside parties to supply the required maintenance services.

Computer equipment and systems are increasingly complex and the rate of change is rapid. For smaller businesses, Computer needs should be contracted to third party providers and as the business grows, this function can be taken 'in-house', at a cost. It is sometimes more efficient and effective leasing networks, servers and the like that purchasing and maintaining them yourself. It is also complicated and best left to specialists.

Payroll

Paying staff members timeously and correctly is critical. Payroll matters are highly confidential and they easily become quite complicated as they easily involve multiple Labor Laws. Payroll can cheaply be outsourced to professional providers who have the latest Payroll software and near expert skills to manage this activity effectively. Employees generally feel happier with outsourced payroll, than in-house payroll.

Policies, procedures, and rules

Every business has policies, procedures and rules. These are used when making certain decisions or they act as guidelines for conducting business and decision-making. These are operationalized by staff and apply to all parties operating within the business. Policies, procedures and rules should be simple. Ideally they should be written down and communicated to all staff members.

- Policies are 'guidelines' that assist decision-making. For example, it may be a policy to not accept returns / products that a customer has already used. However, sometimes products are accepted back under special circumstances and these 'special' circumstances are defined.
- Procedures are detailed 'instructions' on how to perform an activity. For example, equipment has a set operating procedure that cannot be changed and that needs to be adhered quite strictly.
- Rules are explicit 'commands' regarding what actions may or may not be taken. For example, production staff must wear protective clothing. This rule is strict.

Managing your finances

Financial activities usually involve managing the business's finances and they broadly include;

- Providing accurate and relevant financial and statistical information and metrics to the business owners, executives and managers so that performance measurement, analysis and management activities can occur.

- Recording all financial transactions using an accounting system so that financial data is represented in a format recognized by the authorities who require this data to calculate and collect their taxes.
- Complying with all statutory requirements such as submitting financial statements to the tax authorities, processing Income Tax / VAT correctly, calculating and paying over the relevant Payroll taxes, insurances and related contributions.

Recording transactions

This involves recording and accounting for every financial unit that the business handles. There are some excellent computerized systems available that simplify accounting activities considerably. Accounting aims to record every financial transaction of the business and categorize these numerous and varied transactions into specific groups which, once processed offer some meaningful information. Typical accounting records will involve recording and maintaining transactions. These can be categorized as follows:

Source documents identify the original source of a financial transaction, such as:

- Sales orders, Sales invoices, delivery notes etc   for all products sold
- Customer return documents
- Purchase orders, contracts, invoices from suppliers for all goods purchased
- Bank statements, deposit slips, Credit card statements
- Payroll records and summaries

- Petty cash and Expense Report related documents like receipts and vouchers

Ledgers, which record details such as:

- Debtors ledger (monies owing to the business)
- Creditors ledger (monies owed to other businesses)
- Fixed asset ledger (a detailed of all assets owned and used by the business including depreciation rates, accounting 'book' values etc)
- General ledger (any other records required by the business)

Financial statements, including:

- Income statement / Profit & Loss (records sales, cost of goods sold, overheads, other income and profit and loss)
- Balance sheet (records all assets owned and all debts owed by the business)
- Cash-flow statement (records the source and application of historical cash)
- Cash-flow forecast (records the source and application of future cash)

Management reports which include a lot of financial data but also data from key areas of the business which assists managing the business as this data is designed to measure efficiencies and performance. Examples might include;

- Units of production, possibly broken down into each product produced
- Units of time for labor and machine outputs and costs of production
- Units sold by product, product family, by Customer, by geographical location etc

Designing a record keeping system

It is recommended that an effective record-keeping and accounting system should:

- Be as simple as possible
- Be as logical as possible
- Be cheap to set up and maintain
- Be easy to maintain and keep current
- Be flexible enough to accommodate changes
- Satisfy all statutory requirements
- Provide all key financial information

It is important that the system provides accurate and current financial information that can be used in the decision-making process. Care and planning should be taken to design a system that is tailor-made to the way your business operates. Examples may include:

- Processing sales transactions into various product ranges or families so that you can analyze sales (sales fluctuations, comparisons with other sales periods, most popular products sold, seasonality, largest customers, selling-price changes)
- Processing purchases into similar product ranges or families for the same purposes of analysis (cost of goods sold for each individual product, gross profit margins for each individual product, seasonality or trends, largest suppliers, changes in costs).
- Listing each product sold into an inventory system that allows for inventory analysis (perform stock-takes, identify outstanding deliveries, plan future purchases, and analyze price increases).

- Processing payroll costs so that detailed reports can be made for labor costs (time worked per day/week, time spent on an order or project).
- Processing maintenance and repairs as a means of analyzing general maintenance costs (type of repair, frequency of repair, costs).
- Easily identifying all outstanding purchase orders for goods yet to be delivered.
- Age analysis of monies owing to the business, for example: current, 30 days, 60 days.
- Age analysis of monies owed by the business to suppliers and vendors.

Managers need to determine what the key measurement points are in the business and then design a record keeping system that automatically generates these outputs with the least work. The system will also evolve with business needs, so it needs to be flexible enough to accommodate change.

Bank accounts

Usually these are check accounts but they could include other types of bank accounts such as a call accounts, savings accounts, credit card receipt account, disbursement account, foreign exchange accounts etc. Bank accounts generally require individually appointed signatories with authorized authority levels for paper checks, as well as for on-line banking.

Negotiating and managing business agreements

These generally include agreements between business owners with landlords, suppliers, staff employment contracts and customer contracts. The legal process can be complicated and it is recommended that experienced attorneys draft your business agreements. The specific terms and conditions are usually negotiated between the parties, with or without assistance from attorneys and professionals.

Managing the agreement means ensuring that both parties perform their duties as per the terms and conditions of the contract. Failure to do so my require issuing the defaulting party with a written notice to remedy the alleged breach before matters are escalated.

Crooks come in many disguises

Budgets and targets

It is important to determine budgets and targets in a business. Budgets usually involve assessing how much money one expects to spend over a certain period of time and where it will be spent. Budgets should be written down and frequently compared against actual financial activity in order to determine variances, find reasons for the variances and have management activity that aims for corrective action.

Cash-flow management

This involves managing the source and application of cash on a regular basis, as well as predicting future cash cycles and planning for cash shortfalls or surpluses. Cash is critical to a business. Its source and application need to be managed carefully.

Collecting from debtors

Collecting monies owing to the business requires continual management and control. It is important that all monies owing are collected on time and that appropriate action be taken against parties who can't or won't pay.

Costing

Analyzing costs, usually costs associated with making products and determining gross profit margins are necessary to ensure that profits are being made and to identify how they are being made. Regular costing and analysis are necessary as prices, production rates and processes change and evolve. All these factors have an effect on profitability.

Credit control

This involves determining credit limits and conditions for parties who apply for credit from your business. Usually these are customers who wish to purchase products on account. One needs to analyze the customer in order to establish their ability and willingness to repay debt by obtaining a credit check on the customer and its owners or directors, trade references or a bank report, or even reviewing the customer's financial statements. Usually credit facilities are approved, an acceptable credit limit is allowed and, if necessary, some securities may be negotiated. This might take the form of a personal surety by the business owners or directors.

Management accounts and reports

Management accounts are financial and performance styled reports that are prepared for use and interpretation by management. They are not necessarily the same financial statements compiled by an accountant for tax reporting purposes. Financial records and statements can be represented in a manner of different ways, depending on the purpose.

The purpose of management accounts is to use financial and related information in order to make good business decisions. Management accounts usually include details about specific performance areas that managers wish to monitor and manage. Every business has key activities and touch-points that when measured, give an accurate status report of performance. This information when gathered, analyzed and studied over time reveals trends. These are also helpful management information. Managers need to identify what the key and critical performance areas are in a business, so that these can be measured and shaped into management reports. These reports are also used for group management meetings.

Statutory returns

These are typically template external documents that require completion by the business and usually entail payment of some form of tax, levy or similar contribution. Ensure that you are aware of the various statutory requirements relevant to your particular business. Make sure that returns and payments are complete correctly and made on time.

Taxation

Taxation is a complex area of business and often seen as an additional 'cost' of doing business and the returns and benefits for paying all these taxes often seem little, if any.

The usual forms of taxation for businesses include:

- Income tax applicable to the business, as a result of generating taxable profits
- Income tax applicable to the business owners, as a result of distributions and dividends

- Income tax applicable to all staff (including working owners), as a result of payroll taxes on salaries and wages and bonuses and benefits such as medical, insurance etc
- Withholding taxes that are usually applicable to contractors. Whilst not an actual cost to the business, the business is responsible for collecting, remitting and reporting on behalf of the third party.
- Consumption taxes paid on purchases of goods and services
- Taxes raised on the sale of goods and services
- Value Added Tax (VAT) that requires reporting Inputs, Outputs, Zero and Exempt rated transactions
- Foreign trade related taxes and duties applicable on exports and imports

Tax laws are complicated and changes are frequent. All business owners are responsible for the correct recording, declaration and payment of all taxes.

Chapter 13

SWOT and PEST Analysis

What is a SWOT Analysis?

A SWOT Analysis is a planning tool that should be created and updated from time to time. It graphically represents and visualizes the characteristics of a business or project in a simple format;

- **Strengths**. What makes this business stronger than most of its competitors. What are the differentiators the business should be leveraging and maximizing?
- **Weaknesses**. What are the soft spots in the business that need to be fixed? Weaknesses can quickly turn into Threats.
- **Opportunities**. What near and long-term events could present themselves and what affects would these have for the business? How could changes in the future help the business?
- **Threats**. What catastrophic or near catastrophic events could occur that would seriously harm or kill the business?

As an example I refer to a real life SWOT Analysis I used when I purchased a Removals and Storage business that I then owned and later re-sold. This business is also referred to another Case Study in this book.

Case study – SWOT analysis	
Strengths	**_Weaknesses_**
i. 20 year-old business	i. Trucks are old
ii. Reasonably good reputation	ii. Truck running costs are too high
iii. Good lease agreement	iii. Staff morale is moderate to low
iv. Good location / close to markets	iv. Sales have flat-lined / plateaued
v. Low overheads	v. One major market – residential
vi. Multiple income streams – removals & storage	**vi.** Trucks, staff and assets look worn and 'old'
vii. Currently profitable	
Opportunities	**_Threats_**
i. Upgrade trucks	i. Loss of lease agreement & forced relocation
ii. Improve staff morale	ii. Loss of key staff, especially over purchase phase
iii. Re-brand and build on a tenured reputation	
iv. Offer Fast Free Estimates – One hour	iii. Staff join a Labor Union – increases Payroll costs
v. Offer managed conditional discounts	iv. Trucks park overnight in public parking – vandalism?
vi. Improve image, cleanliness and perceptions	v. Fire damage in the public storage warehouse would be catastrophic
vii. Spend more on selected advertising	
viii. Expand into new markets - truck hire and commercial markets	
ix. Improve sales and ROI	
x. Build Balance Sheet and create 'Value'	

This SWOT Analysis was my planning tool, simplified.

Most of what I wrote into this SWOT Analysis concerning Opportunities was achieved within a year and only one of my Threats materialized. My Landlord decided to redevelop the old building in which we occupied 1,500 m2 (16.500 Sq Ft) and we were given notice to vacate. My storage customers rented most of the floor area we occupied and we had to move about 100 customer storage belongings at our own expense to our new premises. Whilst not catastrophic, it did cost me a lot in financial terms and it was disruptive to business.

A SWOT Analysis can be used for any project, business or event that has multiple facets to it. The SWOT helps in visualizing all the components that have some form of influence over the business or project. It should be updated regularly and it should be referred to near weekly. Visualize and work towards the Opportunities, they will materialize.

One can evolve the SWOT Analysis a step further and give each identified Strength, Weakness, Opportunity and Threat a weighting between 1 and 10. Add the total weighting of each grouping and compare Strengths to Weaknesses and Opportunities to Threats. The higher value that Strengths exceed Weaknesses and Opportunities exceed Threats, the better.

Personal SWOT Analysis

A SWOT analysis should also be completed by each owner, executive or manager and the results should be shared with one another. Honesty, respect and confidentiality is encouraged as this requires sharing ones weaknesses with a group.

The purpose is to build teams and to create team work. If owners, executives or managers know more about each other and capitalize and respectfully work with and around these personal SWOT's, this will build towards a stronger business and cohesiveness.

Uses of SWOT Analysis

SWOT's can also be formulated for many important things that require decision-making or greater understanding such as;

- Competitors
- Products and services
- Suppliers
- Markets

What is a PEST Analysis?

A PEST Analysis identifies Macro type / External factors that may influence a business or project. This include Political, Economic, Social and Technological factors.

Examples of factors that may require consideration include;

Political	Economic
<ul><li>environmental issues</li><li>current domestic legislation</li><li>future domestic legislation</li><li>international legislations</li><li>regulatory bodies and changes</li></ul>	<ul><li>status of domestic economy</li><li>status of global economy</li><li>general taxation trends</li><li>taxation specific to your business</li><li>seasonality and trade cycles</li></ul>

- trading policies and changes - grant funding and initiatives - lobbyists and pressure groups - wars and conflicts - changes in political climate	- customer and end-user drivers - interest rates and trends - foreign exchange rates and trends - crude oil prices - energy prices - water supply - labor supply and unemployment - international trade and monetary issues
Social - demographics - boomers, X & Y generations - social attitudes and trends - media views and influencers - consumer buying patterns - fashion and role models - major social events and influencers - ethnic and cultural factors - religious and spiritual factors - social networking trends - ethical issues	**Technological** - technology trends - replacement technologies - new technologies - maturating technologies - social use of technologies - manufacturing capacities - innovation and creativity - information and communications - technology legislation - technology access, licensing, patents - intellectual property and infringements - global communications and connectivity

Whilst a PEST Analysis seems a little abstract, distant and 'far off' from daily business and projects issues, businesses and projects are influenced by these external forces and trends. Be aware of them and monitor them. They offer opportunities and they may present threats

Chapter 14

Managing owners and partners

When business owners combine their resources into a business or project they generally start with high expectations of the business, themselves and of course, their business partners. Unfortunately, the realities can sometime change and not fully meet these early expectations. Climates for disputes and conflict are easily formed, often to the detriment of the business. Effective business owners need to manage themselves properly, individually and jointly. They should seek advice and assistance from qualified outside parties in preparing, negotiating and maintaining the agreements that will govern them and for professional coaching and mentorship.

> ### *Get paid for what you do, not for what you think you know*

The following basic factors should be considered when managing a business relationship:

- ***The business comes first.*** All decisions should be made with the welfare of the business as top priority. Business owners should not act for themselves personally or collectively. Personal interests are not more important than those of the business.
- ***Be prepared to compromise.*** If you are to meet the needs of a group of people, consensus and compromises are needed. If you are not able to make reasonable compromises, then you will creating undue stress on the structure and it will fragment, with casualties.
- ***Written agreements.*** All agreements between partners should be committed to writing. This can be in the form of

an eMail, letter, working notes, minutes of a meeting or formal attorney agreements. Relying on verbal agreements and hearsay is not a good practice.

- **Regular meetings and minutes**. Hold regular meetings at which minutes should be recorded. These minutes are used to record decisions taken, what tasks and deadlines where collectively agreed to and who is responsible for them. Minutes (or extracts) should be circulated to all parties affected by them, so that activity commences. Meetings can also be attended by a third party, such as an accountant, attorney or similarly experienced and trusted person who can act as a mediator or coach.

- **Define job descriptions, work functions and deliverables**. All partners, executives and manager need to know what is expected of them. Working partners should have clear and written job descriptions so that their deliverables can be monitored and assessed. Silent or non-working business partners need to understand what the limits of their authority and responsibilities are.

- **Financial matters**. All partners need to have a financial commitment to the business. Financial matters are usually the most hotly debated issue between business partners, especially when the business doesn't meet certain financial expectations.

- **Salaries and work benefits**. Remuneration needs to be clearly defined. Remuneration should be market-related and to compensate for risk taken as an owner, capital rewards should be realistic too. Certain jobs carry more authority and responsibility than others, so salaries should commensurate with this. All work-related benefits should be calculated, defined, and recorded.

- **Transparency.** Owners, executives and managers should have transparent, honest and forthright channels for communicating. There should be limited 'politics' and 'smoke and mirrors' between Owners, executives and managers.

Loan accounts

In addition to shares / equity instruments, cash or assets invested in the business by owners are usually accounted for under loan accounts. 'Loan accounts' is an accounting term given to the loan that exists between the business and the business owner. This differs from owning any shares, partnership ratio, as these are equity and not the same as loan accounts.

Loan accounts eventually need to be repaid by the business to the business owner and typically Loan Accounts attract interest rates. Any loan account held by an owner or person in a business needs to have a written agreement which governs that loan. Issues such as repayment dates, interest rates, securities and applicable terms and conditions should be fully recorded and agreed to buy the business and all other business owners.

Sometimes business owners take too much money out of a business, to the point where their loan accounts are in deficit and negative and they owe the business money. Agreements must be in place to manage this eventuality. Negative loan accounts should attract interest to the benefit of the business and the repayment of the loan should be properly managed.

Withdrawing unrealized profits is not recommended.

Proportionate loan accounts

Usually business owners agree to invest proportionate amounts of cash or assets into the company. The proportions relate to the percentage of ownership (equity) that they have in the business. For example, an owner of 50% of the company will be required to put in 50% of the cash, while an owner of 20% will only be required to invest 20%. These proportions should be maintained at all times. It may be necessary for partners to invest additional cash – or even be repaid – in order to maintain the loan accounts in proportion.

Disproportionate loan accounts

Agreements should include provisions that compel owners to sell equity in the business should their loan account balances become disproportional to their equity ratio. This prevents equity owners under-funding on their commitments. Similarly, owners who are over-funded should be repaid before dividends are considered.

Equity and loan accounts: the differences

Equity is the accounting term given to the form of ownership in a business. This could be a partnership ratio or a share/s in a corporation or company. Equity is usually calculated as a percentage. For example: 'John owns a 25% equity in XYZ Corporation.

Loan accounts are different from equity. Loan accounts are a financial loan that exists between a business owner (and any person) and the business. They are created when a person invests assets into a business or project and usually the assets are cash but they can also be in the form of equipment, intellectual property (patents, designs, trademarks, trade names, and brands) and sweat equity.

Loan accounts exclude any monies paid to purchase equity / shares. You will usually pay another owner (the seller of equity) a certain price to purchase equity. This payment normally takes place personally and is not reflected in the businesses accounting books. The change in equity is usually recorded in a Share Register of sorts. For example, shares (equity) on the stock exchange change hands every day. The company knows who bought their shares and the Share Register records the changes.

Dividend policies

Dividends are after tax profits that are 'owned' by the business by due to shareholders in accordance with share ratios. Generally businesses like to retain all / most of their profits to leverage future opportunities, to expand and to reduce third party debt. In new and rapid growth businesses, profits are needed as they are a strategic resource, usually in the form of cash.

Mature businesses that have a long track record and profit history may be inclined to adapt a dividend policy where a high ratio of after tax profits are released to shareholders / owners as Dividends.

Dividends should only be released when the business has surplus cash and there is no predicted shortage of funds in the future. Debts ratios should be very low and liquidity ratios should be high.

Other financial benefits

Owners working in a business must fairly agree and approve any additional financial benefits enjoyed by fellow working owners and managers. These 'other' financial benefits exclude compensation vehicles (salaries, bonuses etc) and include soft benefits like medical insurance, subsidized travel, expense accounts (especially entertainment), cellular phones, use of company vehicles or business assets etc. Usually there are tax considerations on these additional benefits for the recipient and there will be reporting obligations for the business.

Case study : Thieves in suits

There was a technology business employing nearly a thousand members of staff. It was the biggest in its specialized field and was making very good money. One day some new executive managers were appointed by the controlling shareholders and they bought a particular style of management to the business.

Very soon things were changing. Strange boardroom deals took place and things began to decline. After some time, shareholders and auditors realized something was wrong but it was a little too late. These new executives were fired but the shareholders had been ripped off by these clever thieves wearing suits.

Later, the business had to be put up for sale and this gave the new buyer an upper hand in negotiations. Eventually a sale did take place and some shareholders recovered 50 % of their original investment.

These thieves in suits are still out there.

Monies due but not paid

Sometimes the business may not have cash resources available to pay an owner any funds owing. What accountants can do is to capitalize that benefit to his loan account, so that even though he may not have physically received any cash, the transaction is added to his loan account. In this way the business acknowledges that it owes him a certain amount of cash. He should then negotiate a future date for repayment.

Sureties and guarantees issued to third parties

Equity owners, executives and managers may be required to sign personal sureties, or guarantees, on behalf of the business as security for any credit or loan facilities. Agreements should be in place whereby these sureties are given in proportional ratios that match equity ratios, together with a right of recourse between parties.

Sometimes the lender or bank holding the guarantees / sureties may choose to sue and collect from just one party for the full amount. This unlucky person should then have agreements in place with the fellow business owners whereby he or she can seek proportional compensation and restoration from co-guarantors.

It is good practice to retain a record of all sureties that have been agreed to. Often, a surety or guarantee is agreed to and given and then forgotten about. Years later, a creditor may still have a legal right to sue based on the old surety that was given.

Valuing the business

Every-one values businesses differently, that is why stocks fluctuate in value, daily.

It is recommended that for privately owned businesses that owners collectively value and agree on an equity value on a regular basis, at least twice a year or when there are material changes. The valuation should also be influenced by a competent third party.

The purpose of the valuation is to set a fair and reasonable value that can be used as a basis for negotiations between partners when an equity transaction is being considered.

'Key man' life policies (death, disability, or incapacitation)

Owners, executives and key managers may wish to insure each other's lives against death or disability. The purpose of this is to provide a cash payout to the business in the event that a 'key' person to the business is no longer able to contribute to the business. The cash can be used in various ways, such as:

- Buying equity in the business
- Repaying a loan account in the business
- Paying out creditors
- Paying out a disabled colleague who can no longer actively work in the business

Arbitration and disputes

A pre-agreed procedure and process should be in place to cater for resolving any disputes. This should first include an attempt to resolve the dispute or issue by relying on a trusted accountant or attorney to settle matters by way or Arbitration and Mediation.

If Arbitration and Mediation is unsuccessful, then aggrieved parties should be entitled to resort to due legal processes in an attempt to settle the matter. Be cautioned though, legal processes are costly and time consuming. Outcomes are not always as predicted and in most cases the disputes are settled out of court.

Case study : Bad partnerships

There was a successful company that had a number of happy working owners. These owners needed additional funding for an expansion, so they invited one more person to join them bringing his skills and finances as a contribution to the business.

After a short period, disputes between the owners started. The disputes led to mediation taking place, but this was unsuccessful. Legal action soon followed and the business found itself in receivership / provisional liquidation.

After some time and considerable expense, the case eventually had its day in court. The owners were forced to compromise and agree on a few issues and the last owner to join, was forced to leave. Shortly afterwards, more disputes started and two more owners departed. Within a year of asking the new owner to join the business, the business had experienced turmoil between owners and there were significant changes. The business suffered terribly and the root cause was the last owner who was invited to join. He was a 'bad fit' and he caused substantial dissent.

Leaving or joining a business

Agreements should be in place to regulate the actions of owners who wish to leave and for new any owners wishing to join the business. Generally, owners leaving the business are required to offer their shares, loan accounts, etc. for sale – stating reasonable terms and conditions to existing owners. The remaining partners should have a reasonable time in which to accept or negotiate this offer. If no deal is forthcoming, then the seller can offer the same deal to outside parties on similar terms and conditions. Outside parties usually need to be 'approved' and screened by the existing owners.

Owners that are leaving need to be released from any sureties and guarantees they may have given to third parties.

Restraint of trade and confidentiality

Business owners should all be bound by a restraint of trade and confidentiality agreements. These agreements attempt to prevent owners from damaging the business by unfairly competing against them and by divulging sensitive and proprietary information about the business. Non-compete agreements with employees, even key employees are generally difficult to uphold.

Chapter 15

Managing People

The degrees of success or failure for a business are solely determined by the quality of people working in the business.

Senior managers and human resources are responsible for recruiting, keeping, motivating and leveraging the skillsets of employees.

The art of management lies within getting work done through people. Managing requires planning, leading, organizing, and controlling functions with employees being responsible for the day-to-day work activities and actions which entail the making and selling of the business products and services.

Understanding company objectives and goals

All managers and employees should understand why a business does things a certain way. This unified and collective understanding allows for a collective and unified approach to working. If employees do-not know that the business wants to double its sales by 50%, how are they supposed to help management in this collective effort?

Understanding the business products and services

Often, many employees do not know what products and services the business makes and sells. Owners and managers need to train and show employees what the business does so there's some product and service awareness.

Employee communication network

Employees are usually the first people to see or hear of things happening or concerning the business. They are on the ground floor, working in production, talking to suppliers, seeing customers. They see managers make mistakes, they know which employees are messing about and they have friends and relatives working for your competitors and the like. They do not always report this information to their managers, even though there are open communication networks within a business. Managers need to identify and use the positive information in this network.

Employee surveys

Employee surveys are a good communication channel to obtain information, opinions and feedback. They should be used in a safe and confidential manner. Nobody is going to 'spill the beans' if they risk getting caught, so the feedback needs to honored and treated seriously and with respect.

Employees can perhaps be grouped into three working types

Champions   Champions are motivated employees that are organized, willing, have ambition, have potential, they want to learn, they notice and report things to managers, they have work pride, they question certain policies and procedures but suggest alternatives, they resign and leave your business for better opportunities and, generally they add considerable value to a business and make a manager's work day more pleasant.

Cruisers   These employees are average. They do what they
            are told, but not too fast. They watch the clock and
            they want compensation for all overtime, complain
            if workloads are too heavy, they seem to take most
            of their sick leave, they tend to stay with the
            business for long periods and generally, they do
            just enough to stay out of trouble they not to annoy
            their managers. Every business needs some of
            these employees, but not too many.

Takers   Takers cost the business in so many ways. They
            are low performers, they distract other employees,
            they have poor time-keeping, they are often absent
            (with no shortage of excuses), they are
            undisciplined, they are disruptive, they add little
            value and they are contaminants. Get rid of them.

Bad employees make a bad business

Quality of management

Bad managers will ruin a good business. There is no substitute for
good management skills as these are catalysts that leverage the best
feasible output from all the resources of the business.

Invest heavily into management training and development and look
after good managers. They are scarce.

Company communication

Managers should continually communicate with each other and employees. People in a business need to know what is going on and communication makes employees feel included. Some of the business information does spread to competitors, suppliers, and customers, so confidential and sensitive information should be restricted and filtered.

Employees meetings

Managers need to hold regular group meetings with employees to set a communication platform where issues from management and employees can be raised and discussed. This platform improves communication and importantly restricts negative information. 'Town halls' are also great, despite being disruptive as they involves most employees at a time.

Feedback

Feedback needs to fostered and encouraged from employees to managers and between managers and senior managers / owners. Information makes for better decision-making and bottom-up feedback and communication channels often present priceless information.

Motivation

Motivation is the key driver that makes people consistently give their best and poorly motivated employees will deliver poor results.

Factors that can materially influence employee motivation are:

Personal goals and objectives. Motivated people generally have clear and definite goals and objectives, as they know what they want and where they want to go in life. In the work place, motivated employees usually have goals and objectives aimed at improving their career prospects so that they can be promoted to better paying and more respected positions. Employees who have no real goals and objectives will be difficult to motivate. Managers should sit with individual employees and establish what these personal goals and objectives are and try synchronize a career path within the business to try and meet most of these goals and objectives. Because of their size, small businesses realistically offer limited career prospects. However, they do offer exposure to many more facets of business. This level of exposure is not easily offered by larger businesses, which are more structured into departments that have little overlap into other areas of the business. Because the small business is closer to its market, its customers and its suppliers, most or all members of employees will be exposed to all facets of the business.

Financial rewards. To a point the more a person can earn, the better they feel about their career job. More money means a better lifestyle, more benefits for self and family, access to material rewards, security and the like. Managers should identify which key employees they will try to retain in the business and these employees should receive better than average financial rewards, so they will be less inclined to job hunt. However, financial rewards do not always totally motivate employees.

Respect and appreciation. Apart from rewarding financial benefits, employees are motivated by formally feeling appreciated and respected by their superiors and their own staff. They are also motivated by informal respect and appreciation through their positioning with their peers. Positive feedback and communication from managers is highly appreciated by employees and it boosts their ego. The use of job titles that define hierarchy also assists in offering job respect. Treating employees fairly and respectfully is highly important, and unfair and disrespectful behaviors quickly break down relationships and cause dissent.

Working conditions. Nobody enjoys working in an environment that is untidy, messy and disorganized. Even worse is working in an unhealthy or dangerous environment. Managers must pay attention to housekeeping and strive for high standards of occupational health and safety. These high standards will draw a positive response from both employees and clients.

Quality of work tools. Employees cannot be expected to work happily and efficiently and deliver quality goods and services when the equipment and tools they work with are in poor condition, slow, outdated or constantly breaking-down. Working under these conditions becomes unpleasant. Employees become demotivated and productivity and output will slump to low levels. Owners and managers must ensure that the tools required to do the job are of an acceptable standard. Anything sub-standard will produce sub-standard results.

Allowing suggestions. Managers will never know all there is to know. Work procedures, policies, structures, employees and managers need to receive positive criticism, so that changes can occur for the better. Often there are employees who notice failings within systems, procedures and processes and they often have positive suggestions to improve these failings. Managers and owners must be open to positive feedback and encourage it, as it is through this process that better systems, policies and procedures are created.

Need to identify. Most employees need to identify and 'belong' to a group within a business. Not just their formal department or business unit but as individuals with similarities. Employee need to identify with their co-workers, as well as with the culture of the business. Although a business is usually made up of a variety of different people who have different ethnic groupings, beliefs, religions and the like, there are certain common fundamentals to which most people subscribe. The areas that people have in common should be built upon to offer a sense of common identity within the business.

Handling conflict and dissatisfaction. It is unavoidable that managers and will encounter conflict and dissatisfaction. Managers may not be entirely 'happy' with certain employees and their actions and likewise, some employees may feel unhappy with certain issues within the business or a particular situation. A hard-lien 'Hire and Fire' policy does-not promote a happy working environment. Ant business or manager should be confident, mature and invested enough to be fair and honest without compromising work standards and reasonable expectations.

Businesses can handle conflict and dissatisfaction these issues through processes like:

- Performance Reviews
- Disciplinary procedures
- Grievance procedures

The aim of both of these processes is to provide a structured, fair and objective process through which all parties can discuss and present facts pertaining to the situation. These discussions are likely to involve formal meetings and perhaps some investigation into the situation. The outcomes need to be fair and enforceable, with clear outcomes if they are not adhered to. Managers may consider using a labor consultant or specialist to assist in these processes.

If the processes are not managed correctly by the business and managers and according to prescribed and recommended protocols, the procedures and outcomes may be construed as 'unfair'. This could result in a financial penalty or cost to the business if matters are formalized and they escalate to third parties outside the business, like labor lawyers.

Performance Reviews

Performance reviews should be conducted on every person who works in the business, from the most senior to the most junior.

People need constructive feedback as it assists in self-development, goal setting, and achieving better results. Reviews should be done every six months as a minimum and they do-not need to be a long time-consuming process. The process needs to be frank, direct, honest, factual and documented.

Employees want and need to know things like;

- How the business is performing, generally,
- How their department / business unit id reporting, generally,
- Are there any planned increases and/or bonuses,
- How does their manager perceive their individual work outputs,
- What their personal work and career goals and objectives,
- What is their progress towards these goals and objectives,
- How do they compare / rate versus their colleagues,
- What are their career paths, if any,
- What areas do they need to improve on,
- What areas are they really strong at etc?

Senior managers need a Peer Review type of review as this strengthens the management 'team' as each member gets to hear feedback from multiple sources. Managers can be reviewed by their Managers / Direct Superior and Peer Review feedback is also recommended, where it is feasible.

Informal reviews should be a regular, near daily activity in the form of feedback, guidance, coaching and mentoring. People are the businesses biggest asset, so they need to be developed and looked after.

Really poor performers need to be 'let go' and strong, competent, motivated and happy people are what is needed if a business is to be successful.

Training

Training involves the developing of a person's skills and competencies through exposing that person to new information. At birth we have instinctive behavior and little else. It is only through a process of 'training' that we acquire skills and become more adept and competent. It is through this exposure to new information that employees and managers become better at their jobs and thereby assist the business.

Most people desire to improve their personal and career skills. Managers need to survey and understand that training themselves and employees is an important part of growing a business and managing employees.

Training does cost money and the returns are not always tangible enough to quantify into hard dollars. However, the returns manifest in different ways that a mature and skilled manager will see. Staff get better at what they do, there are less errors, through-put times increase, customer satisfaction increases etc.

Do-not 'train' staff with boring and irrelevant content just to meet false training objectives. Sometimes some boring and largely irrelevant training is unavoidable as it is required for risk and compliance purposes, so tell the staff that the training is boring but it is necessary.

Outside speakers and external coaches are a good motivating training resource. Anything that pulls the employees away from their work stations and desks and breaks the daily routine consciously gets the attention, so the climate is ripened for new information intake.

Skills audit

Managers can perform an audit to establish what skills exist within the business through the employees who work there. This audit can take place by assessing all employees Resumes and through using Surveys and investigations. The objective is to identify and quantify who has which skills. This information can easily summarized on a matrix spreadsheet.

The next step is to identify what types of skills are required within the business by determining where the various skills are required and to what level of expertise they are required. Various skills are likely to be required in various departments and business units.

A comparison can now be made between what skills exist in the business and which skills should be acquired in order for the business to operate more effectively. This comparison will reveal weaknesses in skills in certain areas of the business.

After identifying the skills gaps are, a training program can be formulated and /or the skills gap can be reduced by employing appropriately skilled new hires.

Training program

The plan program aims to improve the weak skill levels that have been identified within the business by training targeted employees or groups. The plan should attempt to find sources from which the required training can be obtained, the costs involved, entrance requirements, course duration and so on. Employees requiring the skills are then matched to the required courses in order of priority, target dates are set for training and training needs to be competed and on schedule.

Practically however, managers cannot meet every training need as there is a direct cost for training and additional costs when employees are not working, per se. However, employees truly value being trained and acquiring new skills and this also assists with job satisfaction.

On-the-job training

Most businesses adopt semi-formal on-the-job training programs. Here employees are trained on a daily basis usually at their work stations by managers and co-workers. This kind of training usually means that someone perceived to be skilled at a particular job function shows the newbie employee how the job is done, correcting and coaching until there is sufficient skills transfer.

On-the-job training is a very useful and widely used form of training but the quality of the training can be relatively poor if the trainer is a poor trainer or even not that well skilled.

Management training

Often management positions are awarded to technically competent employees but this does not mean they are or will become really good 'managers'. Management involves broad based skills that include planning, leading, organizing and controlling – each of which requires a certain skill set and not everybody has the ability to become a good manager.

Management skills are tested when the business starts growing or facing problems.

Successful managers are those who train themselves by continually absorbing new information. They honestly evaluate their own performances, they acknowledge and learn from their mistakes, they 'listen' and they are sensitive to feedback and they generally try to improve themselves.

Government initiatives in training and skills development

On local and national levels there are always training related initiatives and incentives. Managers should investigate and make inquiries with their industry associations, labor offices and so on and locate information about such these initiatives.

Chapter 16

Common Business Risks

Business risks come in many forms and are encountered on many fronts. Because businesses operate within dynamic constantly changing environments the types of risk change and so do the probability of eventuality. Businesses are different, even those working in the same industries, so each encounters different situations and risks.

Managers need to regularly take a step back from day to day operational activities and assess the risk environment from a holistic viewpoint. Things can change fast.

Common business risks include;

Poor management and low entrepreneurial flair

Entrepreneurship and management skills are the most important assets for any business. These two skills mobilize all the other resources in the business, such as labor, materials and capital. The greater the entrepreneurial flair and the more effective the management, the better the business and profits will be.

Every business needs different styles of management but all styles need to work together, very well. As a business changes and grows, so the management needs of the business will change. Managers need to adapt to the changing management needs of the business.

Over-reliance on key staff members

No single person should be irreplaceable. Key people can place a business at risk due to their overly concentrated influence and control. Key personnel are usually aware of their importance to a business and some try to entrench themselves and create a 'power base'.

People with really strong skills or abilities are vital to a business, but the business should-not over rely on them. Long term business growth and survival vests with a group of skilled people, not just one person.

Competition

Markets can only support a certain volume of sales and a certain volume of sales can only support a finite number of businesses. Changes in the market are often kick-started by competitors or customers. If a business is not prepared for the effects of a change, it will lose out. Always know your competitors as well as you know your customers.

Lack of information

Quality information is required in order to possibly make quality decisions. Often, the writing was on the wall before managers responded to a situation that was clearly visible earlier on. Every business needs internal information systems that collects data, analyzes it and presents it to management for review and action. The pulse points of every process, business unit, manufacturing activity etc needs to be reviewed constantly as does the external environment which includes the businesses markets, competitors, suppliers, technologies etc.

Product substitution

Product substitution happens when customers find and use alternatives (yet similar) products to your own. Factors that may cause customers to look or find substitutes include price, quality, service and availability. Managers should be aware of which products could be substituted and be replaced with another and safe-guard as best as possible. Take steps to make your product/s more competitive.

Case study: Good product but too soon

A start-up business in a developing country started selling a very good lighting product that was doing very well in developed Asian and Western countries. This product offered substantial savings in electricity consumption and was significantly safer when compared to the current product and technology. Despite all the product differentiators, factual cost savings and additional advantages, the local market just didn't like or embrace this new product. Notwithstanding many efforts and attempts, the new business eventually closed down. Sadly, this was a case of a good product that was ahead of its time in this geographical market.

Life cycles

Every product and service has a period of time after which demand will decrease and if left long enough, demand will fail to unviable levels. A typical product life cycle runs as follows:

- Development or introduction stage
- High growth stage
- Maturity and plateau stage

- Decline stage

Ideally, a product should be kept in its growth and maturity stages for as long as possible. This can be done by making the product appear 'new' by making small or significant changes and leveraging differentiators. Clever marketing also influences perception. However, sooner or later products will require a radical change whereby it essentially becomes an entirely new product.

The life span of a product varies from item to item. Effective business owners should constantly be aware of the life cycle of their products, with an eye to prolonging viable life cycles for as long as possible.

Barriers to entry

Businesses that hold a barrier to entry generally have an advantage as the barrier usually prevents or discourages new competition. Typical barriers might include prohibitively high market entry costs, a legal barrier in the form of licenses or permits, or perhaps specialist technological skills or expertise.

Be cautious entering new markets that have barriers as they could be small and restrictive and not as good or as big as initially thought.

Narrow customer base

Any business that relies on a small number of customers is in a vulnerable position. Any customer attrition has a direct impact on sales and profit. Shrewd customers who realize that they account for a significant amount of your sales and gross profit will attempt negotiating more favorable terms and conditions for themselves.

They will demand better prices, longer credit terms, better quality and better service. No single customer (or small grouping of customers) should be able to materially influence your sales and margins.

Narrow supplier base

Relying on a small number of suppliers puts them in a position of strength and it makes your business vulnerable. Large suppliers may attempt to negotiate more favorable terms and conditions for themselves and they could seek higher sell prices, shorter credit terms, less discounts and so on. Suppliers may collude with each other in varying degrees and strategize, the outcomes being that customers are going to pay more.

Without its suppliers, a business has no products or services to offer. Interruptions in the supply of materials and goods may necessitate higher inventory and this becomes expensive. Spread your supply options.

Consistency

Customers want consistency in products, service, price, delivery and everything that they engage in when transacting with a business. If customers feel insecure or annoyed due to changes in consistency, they often start buying products or services elsewhere. Identify the customer touch-points, set standards and regularly measure and maintain them.

Price wars

'Price wars' generally occur when competitors use product / service prices as a strategy to win more market share, place competition under margin pressure and to 'upset' the market. When one competitor starts a price war, others may quickly follow. Participating in a price wars can get expensive as margins deteriorate and one is not certain when price wars will ease-up and cease. Usually, only larger and well-funded competitors benefit as they can absorb the margin losses at the expense of their smaller competitors whilst they grow market share. Customers also enjoy price wars and they can become the displacement trigger for them to start shopping around and testing competitors and breaking loyalty with your business.

Fluctuations in sales

Large fluctuations in sales will unbalance a business. Sales activities may fluctuate between very low and very high levels and this causes disruption in manufacturing, purchasing, inventory levels, and productivity levels. Ultimately, costs increase and there is uncertainty. Careful quick planning can overcome the effects of widely fluctuating sales, but fluctuations will always impact on a business to some extent.

Seasonality, whilst also disruptive is easier to plan for.

Frequent and volatile price ranges

Margins and profits are determined by taking various selling prices and various costs into account. These values are presumed to remain relatively constant. Sometimes however, variations in cost are so frequent and unpredictable that it is difficult to maintain consistency. A business will often end up sacrificing margins in an attempt to stabilize selling prices and keep customers satisfied. Costs incurred by this strategy are absorbed by the business.

Cash flow and liquidity problems

Cash is critical to any business and without sufficient cash a business cannot trade. Not being able to meet obligations in the normal course of business affects a business's reputation and ratings and prolonged cash shortages can have serious effects. Reasons for cash flow problems can be numerous but if they are they are profit related, then serious corrective action is required in order to avoid a business failure. Managing your cash flow and analyzing its various components are critical. You should always be aware of your cash flow position (planned and actual) and the cycles that affect the business.

Valuations

A valuation is an opinion, hopefully an educated one but rarely an exact one. Businesses own a variety of assets and the cost of an asset and the value of an asset often vary. The value of a liability is probably harder to determine compared to valuing an asset as there is more uncertainty. Costs are easy to determine because they are usually proven amounts paid / payable. Contingent liabilities can become open-ended.

In business, manipulating values has consequences that affect Balance Sheets and Profit and Loss Statements. This also affects tax costs, equity value and a host of other data that is used to make decisions.

Always 'test' valuations and seek different opinions and take a slightly conservative approach.

Banks and lenders

Businesses have strong and weak trading cycles. Weak trade cycles usually mean that cash flows and profits are negatively affected. As a consequence, lenders may be pushed into a conservative position to protect any funds they have invested in the business. This position could include revising or even recalling loans and credit lines and in extreme situations, not honoring issued checks.

It is important to consider the effects on your business if you were suddenly forced to immediately repay all debts, credit lines and supplier credit. For most businesses this cannot be achieved and the business probably faces closure.

Don't conduct your banking with just one institution, spread it around so that influence is diminished. At least have checking accounts with other banks, so that deposits can still be processed in the event of a shut-down by your primary bankers.

Many small businesses have not survived because banks and lenders have summarily changed or withdrawn credit facilities and funding, effectively crippling the business.

Difference between cause and effect

Always try to distinguish between cause and effect eg. Repairing defective goods manufactured in production doesn't solve the problem. Stop making defective goods in the first place is the solution.

Often managers attempt to resolve the effects of a problem but they don't even think about the upstream cause. It is critical to identify and address the cause, the effects will look after themselves and they will come out in the wash.

> ## *Case study : One product, one customer, one supplier, one change and one big hiding*
>
> *A marketing business had been supplying one customer with one product for nearly ten years. The marketing business also purchased this one product from a single manufacture. All round, this business partnership of sorts had worked very well until the day the customer decided he needed an upgraded product as the current one's life cycle had matured and his sales were declining.*
>
> *For various reasons, both the marketing company and the manufacturer decided to cancel their agreement and each sought to independently offer the customer this 'new' product. From working together very well and making good profits together, these two companies now became fierce competitors.*
>
> *The customer was a large corporate and quickly realized that it now had two suppliers competing to supply this 'new' product and it started leveraging this situation by playing the two companies off against each other. Eventually the customer got both suppliers to supply similar products at prices and on terms that left neither supplier with a reasonable profit. Sadly, a long-standing viable partnership had ceased due to greed which had also corrupted common sense.*

Poor productivity

Productivity levels affect every business. No two businesses with the same resources will produce the same results. Productivity plays a huge role in this. Being productive extends beyond being able to do things 'faster'. Businesses must also be able to do things 'smarter'. Productivity levels need to be measured and assessed and goals must be set which are diligently worked towards.

You rarely hear employees asking for more work when they are legitimately under-capacity. Instead, employees will take an hour to complete a 20 minute task. This human behavior is common, but when multiplied across multiple employees, processes and activities it has a significant impact on performance ratios and returns. Achieving even a seemingly small increase in productivity will amount to significant gains over a long period.

Poor costing and pricing

Margins (gross profits) pay for overhead expenses and they contribute heavily to cash flow gains. Margins are determined by accurately calculating (not estimating) costs for products / services costs and then pricing them competitively. Absolute margins can be increased by either selling more volume, increasing the selling price or reducing the unit cost of each product.

Managers who cannot accurately cost products and determine accurate margins place the business at risk. Selling below cost is commercial suicide.

Insufficient reserves

Not all costs occur on a regular basis, some are unpredictable. Prudently, every business should have reserves to meet unplanned costs. Regular provisions and savings should be made and funds should be created for a treasure chest. Even small provisions that are set aside accrue into significant lump sums quite quickly. This form of planning and budgeting assists in meeting 'hits' when they occur.

High staff turnover

The majority of employees make a valuable contribution to any business. Losing or replacing employees creates cost and is also a 'lost opportunity' of sorts. Employees leave your business and take with them certain skills and resources. Some employees join competitors and strengthen them.

Businesses with a high staff turnover can also suffer from low staff morale, low productivity levels, poor customer relations, higher recruitment costs and new hire mistakes. All of this negatively affects the business, managers and colleagues.

Staff turnover attributed to voluntary resignations should ideally be lower than 10 %. This signals a healthy and happy workforce.

Sub-contractors and third parties

Sub-contractors and third parties that supply services and goods to your business should be well managed and controlled through clear, concise and enforceable agreements. Each party should be fully aware of its rights, obligations, rewards, risks and penalties.

A concentration and over-reliance on sub-contractors and third parties creates risk as collectively they can hold a high degree of control over the business. Negotiations may favor the sub-contractors if there is any form of collusion. Sub-contractors also sometimes seem to be less committed when compared to direct hires, for several reasons.

Information breaches

Information regarding your business, managers, owners, employees, suppliers, processes, customers, capacities, price lists, intellectual property and the like is sensitive and highly confidential information. This information can sometimes be passed onto third parties with or without the consent or knowledge of the business and these third parties may use of the information for a variety of reasons, not always positively.

As far as practically possible, steps should be taken to limit internal access and information sharing. Confidentiality agreements, non-disclosure agreements, copyrights and patents are some of the methods by which you can protect valuable business information.

Whilst IT Departments and IT systems are reasonably robust and they can assist curtailing (or at least tracking) the leakage of information, nobody can prevent an employee photographing or video filming his computer screen. This subversive activity is difficult to detect and to prevent.

Good influencers?

Identify the key influencers within your business who may pass or make judgment on any material activity, strategy and decision of the business. The groupies and people around them listen and follow these people and often these influencers have unofficial authority as they are not managers. Their influence could be to the benefit or detriment of the business.

There are also influencers who influence key people like senior managers. How often do you see Personal Assistants having significant influence on the decisions made by their senior manager? Personal relationships and friendships can also influence decisions.

Owner-itis

As a business grows, the systems, processes, structures, working methods and management styles need to adapt. Often founder owners find themselves lacking in skillsets as a business grows but they refuse to 'let go' and delegate and leverage better skilled managers.

This insecurity and need for control eventually stifles business growth and good managers get frustrated and may leave.

Most successful start-ups became successful as founding owners realized the need to change.

Continuity of ownership

Management structures need fresh blood, new ideas and continuity. Businesses need a succession plan whereby the business can continue to trade, either under a new owner or under new management. The good younger performers in the business need to be identified early and they need to be given a clear career path into management. Deadwood and past-prime managers need to be re-settled into other less critical positions or 'let go'.

Bad advice

Needing advice normally means that management is unsure of a certain decision or circumstance and that he or she requires the special skills, experience and expert knowledge of a third party. For important decisions and issues do not rely on the advice of just one party, rather get a second or even a third opinion. These additional opinions may be time-consuming and costly but they always add new dimensions and variables to the decision-making process.

Don't always use the same advisors, auditors, legal reps etc. Mix things up and try new ones to prevent complacency and to get fresh alternatives.

Excessive spending by business owners

Some owners, especially in smaller businesses abuse their businesses by withdrawing too much money out of the business. Excessive spending can take the form of buying luxury cars, expensive vacations, large homes, funding investments and home improvements. Working owners need reasonable, market-related salaries and benefits and additional payments or withdrawals should only come out of profits, after first meeting reasonable reinvestment policies. If businesses are to grow and leverage opportunities, they need cash to achieve this.

Property leases

Generally, property leases can become a risky liability. Retail leases in new property developments should be assessed very carefully as supporting demographics don't always justify the rentals sought by the landlords. Typically, new developments are a form of new business and new businesses usually take time to settle in before they become viable.

Conversely, good leases can become good intangible assets.

Losing good leases

The location of a business is a critical choice, especially for a retail business. Leases are usually for set periods of time and they are controlled by terms and conditions held in a lease agreement which has been negotiated between the business (lessee) and the landlord (lessor).

Good trading sites are generally difficult to secure and new and existing competitors are constantly looking for suitable locations. Competitors are often willing to pay top dollar for proven viable sites and this creates demand and pushes rental rates upwards. A good lease/s also contribute towards the overall intangible value of a business.

Losing a good lease can be a catastrophic loss.

Retail leases and recoveries

Strong retail sites usually command high rentals and they are associated with additional costs by way of recoveries that are levied by the landlord or property managers. Excessive rental costs place an added burden onto a business and can increase the break-even point beyond the sales potential of the business. Ideally, base rental costs excluding landlord recoveries for a retail business should not exceed 25 % of the sales generated from that site.

Site and building works

Interruptions and inconveniences caused by physical obstacles such as road works, site and building works will affect traffic flows and the accessibility to a business. Customers will normally avoid such areas and buy elsewhere. Sometimes these faithful customers are lost forever as they find new businesses that meet their needs.

Enduring even a couple of months of business interruption can cripple a business.

Changes in trade flows

Businesses that are reliant on passing trade are extremely vulnerable to changes in trade flows and patterns. These changes can occur due to re-routed traffic due to road changes, the establishment of new property developments in the area, changes to parking (cost and availability of parking), changes in trading hours, traffic congestion, toll roads and the like.

Contracts and agreements

A well-written contract should be clear and concise. Every party to the contract should be fully aware of its rights, obligations, rewards, risks and penalties. Disputes over contracts frequently occur and attempts should first be made to informally resolve the actual or perceived problem. Typically, timeous mediation and arbitration are good processes and failing this, legal action is the last option.

Disputes eventually cost all the parties concerned and rarely does one party feel entirely satisfied with the eventual outcome. Efforts should be made to reach agreement and this means leaving ego's behind and being open to reasonable compromise.

Sometimes parties are too invested and it is too complicated that legal action does become the only vehicle. Extended legal action does have a habit of softening positions.

Disputes between managers

Disputes between managers do occur. Causes vary from misunderstandings, dishonesty, inequities, different opinions, different management styles and simply not 'liking' the person. Every human relationship requires a degree of tolerance.

Disputing managers become emotional, they can make poor decisions and politics can become a negative ingredient in decision-making. Neutralize management disputes as quick and as best as possible. If needs be, separate the managers so that they don't have to interact with one another. The business comes first and it is bigger than any manager or grouping of managers.

The 'real' legal process

Rarely does a plaintiff or defendant actually benefit from initiating or participating in legal disputes. In reality, legal disputes take a long time to resolve, they are frustrating and progress is slow, surprises are common, legal costs are high and the law is not always certain or clear cut. In the vast majority of cases legal disputes are eventually settled out of court with attorneys performing the role of mediation and negotiation. It is advisable to seek a reasonable settlement in the early phase of the dispute, unless you have the time, funds and desire to use the legal process against another party.

Changes in technology

Technologies in business continually change and it is vital to be aware of these developments and identify which are going to be relevant to your business. Staying abreast with technology does cost, but sooner or later this cost becomes unavoidable as every business needs to update its technologies and processes in order to remain competitive. Identifying the relevant technology changes can be difficult but one needs to get stay abreast and invest into the future.

IT threats

As the world becomes more computerized, so computer systems grow and spread and they affect more and more processes and activities in everyday life, including businesses.

Businesses need robust IT resources to prevent hacking, data breaches, fraud and attacks from malware and spam.

Use of outdated or obsolete fixed assets

Using outdated and near obsolete assets, processes and systems will incur higher costs as well as produce inefficient outputs. The greater risk is the growing gap between this business and competitors who are better equipped and more 'modern'. At some point the business will find itself behind the game and it may never be able to 'catch-up'. Reinvest.

Capacity constraints

Most businesses have capacity constraints. Only so much work can be done in a day. Businesses rarely run at full capacity and if they did for extended periods, they would probably break down. Only really well managed and invested businesses can keep running at high speed without interruption.

All businesses, especially manufacturing-based businesses need to determine what their capacity constraints are and what issues determine and influence the constraint. Many businesses have invested substantial amounts of funds into new projects only to realize later that their break-even point is higher than maximum capacity output.

Too many constraints through-out a business will unbalance it and it will sink to its lowest denominator / weakest link.

Bad debts

Not being paid by a customer really hurts the business, both morale and finances. Bad debts affect cash flow and may they may affect sales budgets too. Bad debts generally occur when a customer is unable or unwilling to pay for the product or service. Whatever the reason, businesses should attempt to negotiate with the customer and attempt to recover something towards the costs incurred by the business. This recovery could include taking the products back, negotiating a repayment plan with the customer or even accepting a lower amount in settlement.

Communication with customers who cannot pay or who are unwilling to pay is important. Keeping doors open and encouraging dialogue always help recovery processes.

Act of God

'Act of God' events include uncharacteristic and low probability events associated with natural events, such as floods, fires, lightning, hail, rock / mud slides, sink holes, gales, hurricanes and tornadoes. These events are usually unpredictable and infrequent. However, when they do occur the disruptions and loss they create are generally severe. It is difficult to plan for these events beyond having a 'recovery' plan that is well thought-out and that is rehearsed on a regular basis.

Bad insurance

Business insurance is a complex subject matter. Being adequately insured is not always easy to achieve but it's important to know exactly what risks you are insured against and what the terms, costs, conditions and amount of cover are available for each category of insurance. Being under-insured or not insured against a substantial claim or loss can be catastrophic.

Taxes

Taxes come in many forms and tax laws, their interpretations and practical execution is not always consistent. Add to this trading in global economies, exports and imports, consumption taxes, VAT, capital gains, transfer pricing and the like and tax matters can get quite complicated.

Remaining compliant is critical as an incorrect tax policy can create a large debt liability and margins can be affected if certain taxes were not raised and collected from contracting parties like customers. Always get clear and high quality tax advice.

Labor unrest

All businesses rely on employees to perform job functions. Labor unrest affects businesses through lower productivity levels and 'lost' production and feelings of distrust and resentment between management and employees can adversely affect working relationships.

Fraud

Fraud is a common finding in business and white collar crime is prevalent. Managers need to audit money flows where-ever possible and they need to have checks and balances in place to prevent collusion and to lower temptation.

Often fraud is in the form of theft of cash or similar instruments, 'back handers' from suppliers and manipulation of costs and prices to filter money out of the business to a colluding external party.

Infrastructural weaknesses

Managers from developed countries take it for granted that macro infrastructure is well developed and reliable. When they have to work globally, especially with developing countries they find it frustrating when power supplies are interrupted, internet speeds are really slow, cell phone signals are weak or lost, businesses don't have web sites, eMail is not a common communication medium etc.

Where possible, businesses should plan to be self-reliant on electricity, at least if only for a temporary period until grids are restored. Without electricity, nothing works.

Globally connected

Globally, markets are becoming inter-connected and easily influenced by global changes. Something big happens in China probably means that similar markets in USA are affected. There is growing pressure to think 'Global' and it is not always easy to differentiate between what is relevant and what is irrelevant. Nonetheless, managers need to track global politics, global societies, global markets, large global competitors, large global customers, large global suppliers and the like as these will be likely market influencers.

Chapter 17

Testing Questions

The business environment changes constantly, so managers should evaluate their business units on a regular basis. It is not always possible to;

- Capitalize on strengths
- Avoid and limit the effects of weaknesses
- Leverage all opportunities
- Avoid threats

It is also impossible to have a 'perfect business', where everything works well and there is no more room for improvement. Most businesses are content to 'survive' and others aim to make good profits for as long as possible.

To assess the general position of a business, managers should be asking themselves questions like;

Owners and executives

1. Do you really know why you are in business?
2. Are you generally very successful in the things you undertake?
3. Are you wise?
4. Are you physically active?
5. Are you mentally active?
6. Can you communicate effectively?
7. Do you really listen?

8. Do you actually 'hear' what people are trying to tell you?
9. Are you realistic?
10. Are you happy with yourself?
11. Can you do any better?
12. Do you want more from life?
13. Do you have clear personal plans for yourself?
14. Are you confident?
15. Are you aware of news, events and worldly things happening around you?
16. Do you know exactly what your personal / household expenses are every month?
17. Do you own a lot of assets?
18. Are you scared to lose money?
19. Do you always repay your debts?
20. Do you have good instincts or gut feel?
21. Do you usually try your best?
22. Is your best usually good enough?
23. Do you like to learn?
24. Do you actually implement and follow through with things you have learnt?
25. Are you well liked?

Results

'Yes' answers indicate a personality with high probability of being successful in business; a general awareness and sensitivity to risk, money, economics and the business environment; a strong character who keeps trying; someone who is instinctive, active and pro-active.

Business structure

1. Are some employees <u>always</u> busier than others?

2. Do some employees always legitimately complain about having too much work?

3. Are certain departments / business units always giving problems?

4. Is work output usually late for some reason?

5. Do departments or business units frequently conflict or fight with one another?

6. Do any departments or business units regularly complain about the other?

7. Do any departments or business units cause problems for any other department?

8. Is overtime frequently worked?

9. Has the business structure been changed at all in the last year?

10. Have any large processes been reorganized recently?

11. Is the business growing?

12. Are customer complaints rising?

13. Are suppliers fulfilling Purchase Orders on time?

14. Is head count growing rapidly?

15. Is work getting more complicated and harder to do?

16. Are there more projects in progress now compared to six months ago?

17. Are new work processes being used?

18. Is there a recent Organization / Resource Allocation Chart for all employees to look at?

19. Is work often re-done or duplicated?

20. Is your business's structure very different from that of your competitor's?

21. Are work activities generally poorly organized?

22. Is there a mood of disruption and possibly 'chaos' in the business?

Results

'Yes' answers indicate: a need for a revised business structure; work functions may need to be reorganized; work functions and resources are not balanced; there is conflict between departments; certain employees are under pressure, while others are comfortable; customers will be lost soon unless matters are corrected and leadership needs to regain control.

Management and employees

1. Do all the employees know exactly what products / services the business sells?
2. Do all the employees know what the business does?
3. Do all employees know the businesses Mission Statement, goals and objectives?
4. Do most of the employees know who the biggest customers are?
5. Do most of the employees know who the biggest competitors are?
6. Does every employee know what job function he or she must perform?
7. Do employees frequently socialize with each other outside of work?
8. Do employees feel proud of the business they work for?
9. Have most members ever been managers in other businesses?
10. Do all managers have a college education?
11. Do managers frequently meet and positively discuss the business?
12. Do managers keep minutes or notes of meetings for future follow-up?
13. Do all managers know what the business plans to achieve in the next year?

14. Do employees, departments and managers help each other out?
15. Can most managers be changed around to manage other departments?
16. Is employee turnover less than 10% per annum?
17. Do managers regularly make use of consultants and external experts?
18. Do managers train employees regularly?
19. Is the office 'grapevine' or informal communication network generally quiet?
20. Does the business generally run smoothly?
21. Do managers recognize good employee performance?
22. Do managers reward employees who perform well?
23. Do employees appear to be happy and content working in the business?

Results

'Yes' answers indicate: the business is well managed; management skills are quite broad; there is depth in management; management and employees work well together; employees generally have the business's interests at heart; employees are generally motivated; employees are well informed and enjoy working with the business.

Business is a team effort. A weak team means a weak business

Sales marketing

1. Does the business sell a large volume or quantity of products?
2. Does the business sell a large range of different types of products?

3. Have any new products been added to the product range in the past six months?
4. Would the business survive if it stopped selling its two most popular products / services?
5. Does the business sell to a large number of customers?
6. Would the business survive if it lost 25% of its customers?
7. Would the business survive if it lost its top 5 customers?
8. Would the business survive if it decreased selling prices by 25%?
9. Would the biggest customers accept a price increase of 20%?
10. Do most customers return and purchase from the business gain?
11. Do you know what your customers do with your products?
12. Does the business have less than ten direct competitors?
13. Can the business significantly influence the market in any way?
14. Do only a few new direct competitors enter your market/s from time to time?
15. Does the business know which competitors pose the greatest threat?
16. Does the business know why these competitors pose a threat to the business?
17. Is it relatively difficult for new direct competitors to start in this industry?
18. Are competitor informational files updated with new information at least once a month?
19. Have sales volumes increased more than 30% over the past two years?
20. Do you measure the success / ROI of advertisements?
21. Does the business regularly get new customers?
22. Are sales employees dedicated, loyal and effective?
23. Are your sales employees focused on their jobs?
24. Are sales employees receiving regular training?

25. Do you survey your customers?
26. Are you your customer surveys representative and meaningful?
27. Do your customer surveys consistently yield above 95 % satisfaction ratings?

Results

'Yes' answers indicate: a large product range exists, which allows for flexibility; there is a large customer base, so individual customers don't have too much power or influence over the business; actions caused by competition are manageable; competition can't easily upset the market; markets are relatively stable and growing; competitors are closely monitored and analyzed; the business can recover from sudden market changes; prices are not highly sensitive to competition; sales employees are working in the best interests of the business.

Treat the customer like a king, but don't become a slave

Manufacturing

1. Does manufacturing generate much waste material that cannot be used again?
2. Does it take longer than a week to make a complete product?
3. Do manufacturing employees spend a lot of time away from their work stations?
4. Do manufacturing employees walk around much?
5. Do manufacturing employees frequently take toilet breaks, visit and talk to one another?
6. If there was 20% less employees, would output remain unchanged?

7. Are there any processes which only one person knows how to perform?
8. Is there any equipment which only one person knows how to operate?
9. Are employees unable to swop-out and work at different work stations?
10. Are you still following the same work processes from 12 months ago?
11. Are you still using the same equipment you used 12 months ago?
12. Do some work stations always have more unfinished work than others?
13. Does equipment frequently break down?
14. Is overtime frequently required to meet normal demand?
15. Is there high absenteeism from blue collar employees?
16. Are quality standards declining?
17. Are reject rates increasing?
18. Would there be any problems if manufacturing needed to suddenly increase by 30%?
19. Have manufacturing managers previously worked as managers in other manufacturing plants?
20. Do manufacturing managers have conflict with employees over manufacturing problems?
21. Are work processes documented?
22. Are Standard Operating Procedures and Manual inaccurate and outdated?
23. Are work stations generally untidy and messy?
24. Are there frequent work related accidents or similar threatening 'incidents'?

Results

'Yes' answers indicate: inefficient work processes; low productivity; poor management skills; over-reliance on certain key employees; a low priority for implementing new and better work processes; poor flexibility, can't easily react to changes; low skills depth with a need for job development.

Good employees are hard to find.

Purchasing, quality and logistics

1. Are written purchase orders issued for everything that the business purchases?
2. Does the business know what has been ordered but not yet delivered?
3. Can 30% of the suppliers be easily replaced?
4. Are price increases from suppliers easily predicted before they occur?
5. Does the business know where the suppliers get their products?
6. Do managers know the most economic quantity when purchasing goods?
7. Do all suppliers have similar prices, terms and conditions for the goods supplied?
8. Do managers compare prices, terms and conditions from new global suppliers?
9. Is the purchasing manager's work independently audited?
10. Does the purchasing manager declare all gifts from suppliers?
11. Can goods only be purchased with the written consent of management?
12. Are goods ordered actually delivered?
13. Are goods delivered physically inspected and counted?
14. Has all measuring equipment been calibrated in the last six months?
15. Can random samples in stores be traced back to the original suppliers?

16. Are there written quality policies and objectives?

17. Are there accurate quality reference samples for each of the products sold / purchased?

18. Is the management confident that the manufactured products are not defective in any way?

19. Are all goods purchased compared with quality reference samples?

20. Do managers know what causes the majority of manufacturing rejects?

21. Can it be established how many rejects were made on a random date four months ago?

22. Is a first-aid kit and a trauma procedure in place?

23. Do managers know who has keys / access to the premises after hours?

24. Does management know who can reprogram the security or alarm system?

25. Do the premises look neat and tidy?

26. Are things easily found?

27. Are products always delivered to customers on time?

28. Are goods always collected on time?

Results

'Yes' answers indicate: well managed purchasing methods; a wide supplier base where no supplier has any control or influence over the business; an awareness of purchasing fraud; healthy competition between suppliers; quality awareness; the use of tests and quality procedures; reliable records tracking rejects and the causes thereof; reliable records tracking goods bought and sold; good housekeeping with presentable, secure and well-managed premises.

Administration, HR and IT

1. Can random records from two years ago be found easily?
2. Are correspondence, records and files rarely lost?
3. Are all computer software packages legal and licensed versions?
4. Are computers regularly backed-up?
5. Are copies of computer back-ups kept safe at an offsite location/s?
6. Has insurance cover been reviewed in the past six months?
7. If all records were destroyed in a fire, would back-up records exist?
8. Do all employees have written employment contracts?
9. Do all employees have written job descriptions?
10. Is there a written grievance and disciplinary procedure?
11. Is there someone who represents employees on labor-related issues like grievances?
12. Is the business up to date with all the latest labor legislation?
13. Are all sales records for the past six months neatly filed?
14. Have customer records been updated in the past three months?
15. Can it be easily proven in writing which employees were not at work last week?
16. Is the average number of private phone calls made each day known?
17. Is it certain that no documents, information or records have been stolen?
18. Do only authorized employees see and deal with confidential information?
19. Is there an accurate register for all assets taken off the premises?
20. Are the dustbins checked for hidden confidential information or even assets?

21. Are regular employees surveys performed?
22. Are regular employee reviews performed?
23. Are IT audited by external auditors?
24. Are employees happy with HR department?

Results

'Yes' answers indicate the presence of a managed documentation system ;an awareness of confidentiality and security; evidence of reliable record-keeping; adherence to the elements of basic labor laws; a level of control over correspondence and a functional HR activity.

Finance

1. Have product costings been reviewed on all products within the past six months?
2. Do managers know which two products give the biggest gross profit margins?
3. Has the weighted gross profit percentage changed in the past six months?
4. Do managers know why gross profits have changed in the past three months?
5. Do managers know what sales are required to break even?
6. Can finance team easily calculate profits or losses for the week, month, quarter and year?
7. Are all statutory returns and associated payments up to date?
8. If overheads increased by 35%, would the business still make a profit?
9. Are sales, payments and deposits banked every day?
10. Does senior management personally analyze every page of the bank statements?

11. Do managers know exactly how much debt the business has?

12. Do managers know exactly what assets the business has?

13. Is there an accurate Asset Register?

14. Is the business solvent?

15. Is there a record of all sureties or guarantees that been signed for by owners / managers?

16. Are there copies of all agreements and contracts entered into by the business?

17. Do managers know how much money will be needed by the business three months from now?

18. Does every customer pay for everything they get from the business?

19. Would the business survive if it had no sales for a month?

20. Would the business survive if it had no sales for two months?

21. Is the work done by finance team audited by an external auditor?

22. Are business checks kept in a secure and restricted place?

23. Digital signatures are not permitted to sign checks?

24. Customer credits and refunds are independently investigated?

25. Payroll records are cross-checked to payments and source documents by third parties?

Results

'Yes' answers indicate: an ability to survive a cash flow shortage; an ability to repay all debts; an understanding of costings and gross profits; an understanding of break-even analysis and its variables; the presence of basic financial controls and a degree of planning.

Chapter 18

Post Trauma

Business failure is traumatic. It places great emotional and financial pressure on all parties who relied on the business for income and security. There is fallout, stress and tension all around.

If business failure seems to be a possible eventuality then consider the following, mainly personal points;

Be realistic

There is a fine line between being committed to the business and being stupid. If outsiders are advising you to change and you refuse to listen, then you must accept the risks you are taking and the possible outcomes. If things are looking really bad, then realize where you are and choose to either to see the business through at all costs or start planning your next move.

Do not hope that some miracle will happen and things will end like a fairytale. In most cases, you have to take the responsibility, and the action, yourself. If the writing is on the wall, react. Do-not procrastinate.

Don't throw good money after bad

Many managers and owners make the mistake of committing more money to a business or project that has little or low probability of surviving. This mistake is done in the belief that things will eventually improve and return to normal. A business or project that is in trouble usually starts off by needing more money and failing to meet budgets and targets. This pattern plays itself out again and again. At some point you have to realize that a difficult decision has to be made. In difficult times you need to use your cash very wisely, if you are to stand a reasonable chance of making a comeback.

Get advice

Get advice from an accountant, consultant, bankruptcy attorney, or someone who has the experience to summarize your financial position and possibly map a feasible way forward. You might already know the intuitive answers, but confirmation from a third party can help when difficult choices have to be made.

Have a nest egg

Without cash, the chances of riding-out the failure and recovering are weakened. At these difficult times most credit lines, both business and personal are either withdrawn or fully utilized. Nobody will lend you money easily. Without money you cannot pay for your normal personal monthly expenses, nor can you start rebuilding or executing your next move.

Ensure you have enough cash to keep your personal show going for at least six months.

Limit your personal risks

In business it is prudent to safeguard personal assets and avoiding issuing personal sureties and guarantees. Obtain legal advice for the most effective vehicles to leverage and safeguard your assets in trusts, corporations and consider off-shore and trusted nominees.

Get some support

During times of business / project failure the need for support is very high. Professional support in the form of information, advice and counselling and also emotional support from friends and family. Take care of your health, your relationships and the people around you and avoid substance abuse. Try and stay focused.

Handle creditors carefully

Some creditors are approachable and are prepared to assist, whilst others can make things worse. Some creditors are hard liners and managing this can become very difficult. Try and manage creditors as best as possible. Sometimes it is easier to seek legal assistance from an attorney and accountant who can negotiate on your behalf. Alternatively, using legal remedies such as bankruptcy might be the only viable option left.

Prepare for rumors and stories

With business / project failure there are stories. These vary from factual or part-factual to downright untrue. The sources of these stories will be competitors, employees, colleagues, suppliers and just about anyone who has had a relationship with the business.

Be prepared to hear the stories and tell your version too.

Things *will* get better

Given time, things *do* get better. Business owners must accept that they have little control over their business once it fails. This period can be extremely difficult and testing. It passes and with time things get better. Life goes on; employees get new jobs; creditors write off debts. People move on and so should you.

IAN JUUL

The best businessmen have often failed more than once in business

www.ingramcontent.com/pod-product-compliance
Lightning Source LLC
Chambersburg PA
CBHW051902170526
45168CB00001B/211